Reminiscences

of

Mr. Frank E. Sublett, Jr.

Member of the Golden Thirteen

Copyright © 1989
U.S. Naval Institute
Annapolis, Maryland

Preface

In the first few months of 1944, 16 black enlisted men went through officer training at Great Lakes, Illinois. Of the group, 12 were commissioned as ensigns and one as a warrant officer. They were the Navy's first black officers. Collectively, the group has come to be known as the Golden Thirteen. In the autumn of 1986, the Naval Institute began an oral history project involving the eight surviving members of the group. This volume represents the life story of one of those eight men, Frank E. Sublett, Jr.

Race has not been much of an issue in Frank Sublett's life, because he deals with people as fellow human beings rather than as members of a particular group. His philosophy is one of live and let live, and it has served him well. Mr. Sublett is a likable individual, one who becomes a friend from the time one first meets him. He is a thoroughgoing gentleman and a man of dignity; those qualities doubtless were factors in his being chosen from the Navy's enlisted ranks to undergo officer training.

Following officer training, Frank Sublett served briefly at the Naval Training School at Hampton, Virginia. This was one of a series of what he considered make-work assignments. Later he served on board a patrol craft, a yard oiler, and with a stevedore battalion on Eniwetok. Though he relished his time in the Navy, he is still sorry that he and the other members of the Golden Thirteen were not given the opportunity to serve in combatant ships. Even so, theirs was a highly significant accomplishment. The thousands of black officers who have come after them look back to honor the Golden Thirteen who paved the way.

Much of Mr. Sublett's life has revolved around Lake Michigan's North Shore area, near Chicago. With the exception of his years in the Navy, he has spent nearly all his life there, living and working as a good citizen. An athlete in high school and college, his education was cut short by World War II. In the postwar period, faced with the need to support a growing family, he began a career in the automobile business. Since retirement from that field, he has become a professional model. Probably the biggest regret of Mr. Sublett's life is that circumstances prevented him from making a career of the Navy.

In the transcript that follows, both the interviewer and interviewee have done some editing in the interests of clarity, accuracy, and brevity. The original verbatim transcript is on file with the Naval Institute. The transcription was done by Ms. Deborah Reid and Ms. Joanne Patmore of the Naval Institute's oral history staff.

                                            Paul Stillwell
                                      Director of Oral History
                                      U. S. Naval Institute
                                      May 1989

FRANK ELLIS SUBLETT, JR.

Birthplace

Murphreesboro, Tennessee, 5 March 1920
   (raised in Glencoe, Illinois)

Education

New Trier High School, Winnetka, Illinois, 1934-38
University of Wisconsin, 1938-39
Northwestern University, 1939-40
George Williams College, 1940-41

Military Service

Enlisted in the U. S. Navy, July 1942
Completed U. S. Naval Training School in Hampton, Virginia,
   December 1942, machinist's mate second class
Sent to Boston's section base machine shop, January 1943
Aboard auxiliary patrol craft in Atlantic Ocean operating
   sonar for detecting submarines, February 1943
Boston machine shop, machinists' mate first class, May 1943
Entered officer indoctrination school in Great Lakes,
   January 1944
Commissioned as an ensign, 17 March 1944
Instructor in small boat handling and military bearing
   U.S.N.T.S., Hampton, Virginia, May 1944
Auxiliary ship yard patrol, and executive officer
   yard oiler, Twelfth Naval District, San
   Francisco, July 1944
Instructor, Great Lakes, Illinois, prevention of venereal
   disease, March 1945
Pacific Fleet officers' pool, Oahu, Hawaii, June 1945
Promoted to lieutenant (junior grade), July 1945
Logistics Support Company, Iroquois Point, Hawaii, August
   1945
Executive officer, Logistics Support System, Naval Supply
   Depot, Eniwetok, June 1945
U. S. Naval Reserve, inactive duty, 23 May 1946

Employment

Foley Buick, Wilmette, Illinois, 1946-51
Manager at Grant Dean Buick, Highland Park, Illinois,
   1951-80
Professional model, Emelia Lorence Model and Talent Agency,
   Chicago, Illinois, 1980-present

Family

Two daughters, Rosanne and Nicole, and two sons, Frank III and Michael

Authorization

The U. S. Naval Institute is hereby authorized to make available to individuals, libraries, and other repositories of its choosing the transcripts of two oral history interviews concerning the life and career of the undersigned. The interviews were recorded on 8 October 1986 and 21 July 1988 in collaboration with Paul Stillwell for the U. S. Naval Institute.

The undersigned does hereby release and assign to the U. S. Naval Institute all right, title, restrictions, and interest in the interviews. The copyright in both the oral and transcribed versions shall be the sole property of the U. S. Naval Institute. The tape recordings of the interviews are and will remain the property of the U. S. Naval Institute.

Signed and sealed this 15TH day of MAY 1989.

Mr. Frank Sublett

Sublett #1 - 1

Interview Number 1 with Mr. Frank E. Sublett, Jr.

Place: Mr. Sublett's home in Glencoe, Illinois

Date: Wednesday, 8 October 1986

Interviewer: Paul Stillwell

Q: It's a pleasure to be with you this morning, Mr. Sublett. Just to begin at the beginning, perhaps you could tell me something about your parents, your family background, and your early years before you got into the Navy.

Mr. Sublett: I was born March 5, 1920, in Murfreesboro, Tennessee. My parents moved to Highland Park, Illinois--in the Chicago area--when I was about five years old.* After just about a year in Highland Park, our family moved to Glencoe.** As a matter of fact, I grew up in the house right next door to this one. I went to school here in Glencoe, first through eighth grades. I went to high school in Winnetka, which is about four miles away.*** I participated in all the athletic programs that were available.

---
*Census figures for Highland Park: 1920--6,167; 1930, 12,203.
**Census figures for Glencoe: 1930--6,295; 1940--6,825.
***Census figures for Winnetka: 1930--12,166; 1940--12,430.

Sublett #1 - 2

Q: What sports were you in?

Mr. Sublett: I specialized in football and track and did pretty well in those. In football I got some assistance to go to the University of Wisconsin in 1938 and played a little ball up there.*

Q: Don't be modest.

Mr. Sublett: I didn't excel in any particular area there, but I did play. It was a pretty good experience.

Q: What position did you play?

Mr. Sublett: I played end. At that time we were defensive and offensive. There were no split ends and wide receivers and that sort of thing. I didn't play more than '38 and '39. I had a little problem with grades, so I had to split from that. In track and field I was involved in the discus and the shot put.

Q: You're a good-sized man now. How soon did you achieve your physical maturity?

Mr. Sublett: When I left high school, I was 185 pounds and

---

*University of Wisconsin, Madison, Wisconsin.

Sublett #1 - 3

went up to about 220 my freshman year in college. I'm smaller now because I don't need it. Under the advice of doctors I dropped down to about 200. I slimmed down quite a bit when I attempted to get into the Air Force, before I went to the Navy.* At that time there was not an opening, because only one field was available for black pilots, the one at Tuskegee, Alabama.

Q: Before we get to that, I wonder if we could talk about your growing-up years and your parents?

Mr. Sublett: My mother still lives.** My dad died in September 1956.*** My mother did domestic work here on the North Shore, in Highland Park and in Glencoe.**** She was a companion to a lady who just passed in the last couple of years, so now Mom is not working, but she still lives and is doing pretty well. My dad was a milkman, he was a railroad porter, sold insurance, and I think at one time he was a chauffeur. I think his last job was with the North Western Railroad.*****

---

*At the time the organization was officially the U.S. Army Air Forces; in 1947 it became the U.S. Air Force.
**Mr. Sublett's mother's name is Rosa S. Taylor.
***Mr. Sublett's father was Frank E. Sublett, Sr.
****The North Shore refers to the well-to-do suburbs north of Chicago, near the shore of Lake Michigan.
*****Chicago and North Western Railway.

Sublett #1 - 4

Q: How did your family fare during the Depression?

Mr. Sublett: At that time, my mom and dad split up and divorced.* I stayed with Mom and also spent some time with an aunt and uncle that lived here in Glencoe. During the Depression, I don't recall too many problems. I recall that I used to go up to a tearoom that my uncle worked at, and I used to do odd jobs there. I was a busboy, or a cleaner-upper, before going to school in the morning. It wasn't a necessity, but I suppose it was part of my bringing-up. I also cut lawns and did odd jobs, as many of the kids did around there. I had a bank account.

Q: So early on, you had the idea of earning your living.

Mr. Sublett: It helped a lot to get to work early in the morning and sometimes on Sunday afternoon, because I spent a lot of time down here at the beach, either swimming or fishing. And I used to go with my uncle on fishing trips to Wisconsin maybe once or twice during each summer.

Q: Did you have any brothers and sisters?

Mr. Sublett: I have one sister, Frances, who is a year and a half younger than I. I was always busy playing baseball

---

*The divorce was in 1931.

Sublett #1 - 5

or some other sport. My home life was very good, absolutely one of the best.

Q: How big a factor was religion in the family life?

Mr. Sublett: Just average, I would say. I went to Sunday School every Sunday, and I participated in the Christmas and Easter programs that they had for the youngsters. There was no heavy influence in any particular type of religion. I've gone to the Baptist church when they had one here. I went to the Methodist church, which is still here. I've been to the Catholic church probably more than any other church that I've attended in my life. However, I was married by an Episcopalian.

Q: How good a student were you in grade school and high school?

Mr. Sublett: In grade school I was maybe a shade above average. In high school, in some subjects I was above average. As a matter of fact, I graduated with a high average in algebra and mathematics. Otherwise, I was maybe just slightly above average.

Q: Did your mother put emphasis on education as a key to success?

Sublett #1 - 6

Mr. Sublett: My mom did not push me in any way at all. The environment here creates a situation where you just go to school. There is no thinking of dropping out. What would you do if you did, anyway, out here? I lived a good, clean life growing up as a kid here, as most of us did. I was never involved in any activities that would be embarrassing to my family or to myself. But Mom has always figured that I knew best, and she'd let it go at that. Therefore, I never gave her any trouble, and she'll say that today. I'm proud of that.

Q: Were you in integrated situations all along?

Mr. Sublett: All along it's been that way. When I grew up here, there were very few black families. I was probably many times the only black kid in my class. And then, when I graduated from high school, I think there were probably only three or four in my entire class of 539. So I grew up in an atmosphere that didn't involve any prejudices. I'm sure they were there, but I didn't encounter any problems at all.

Q: They weren't overt at all?

Mr. Sublett: No. That's right. I didn't have to think

about something that was off-color. I was accepted, and maybe my attitude had a lot to do with it.

Q: What sort of attitude did you adopt?

Mr. Sublett: Just live and let live. I wasn't looking for anybody to give me any trouble, and I wasn't giving anybody else any trouble. It didn't cross my mind. I was dark skinned and somebody else was white skinned; it didn't matter to me. We played together and did other things together.

This neighborhood is still mixed. I have a white neighbor on this side and a black neighbor on that side of me, so it's the same way. Directly across the street are whites.

I didn't have any problems in school, in or outside of school, none at all.

Q: You were luckier than many of your generation.

Mr. Sublett: I was fortunate, I would say. Absolutely. Because I have read about problems that people have had, and I have been very fortunate not to have run into those situations. There might have been prejudices. They're all over the world. But I did not get involved with them somehow.

Sublett #1 - 8

Q: Did you pull your grades up after you stopped playing football at Wisconsin?

Mr. Sublett: Slightly. I went down to Northwestern University for a couple of semesters in '39 and '40.* I was initiated into Kappa Alpha Psi fraternity, Theta chapter, at Northwestern in May 1940. Then I switched to George Williams College in 1941 and '42.** I didn't play any more football. My grades did come up, yes, after concentration. I didn't get involved in track anymore, either. I gave up all those things except on the outside. I didn't do any more in school.

Q: Did you have any career goals at that point?

Mr. Sublett: No, at that time I didn't. As a matter of fact, in college I was taking a liberal arts course with a slight intention in the back of my mind to get involved in a premed course. That was the only inkling of a future anticipated. At George Williams College, it was more or less a teachers' school, YMCA work, education.*** As I look back now, I should have probably gotten into the business course and would have fared much better in today's

---
*Northwestern University, Evanston, Illinois.
**George Williams College was then at East 51st Street on the south side of Chicago.
***YMCA--Young Men's Christian Association.

world.

Q: But you had to prepare for the world of that day.

Mr. Sublett: At that time, I figured medicine would be good, but I started out on a liberal arts course and didn't do too badly with it. I liked it, as a matter of fact.

Q: What subjects did you do especially well in? Again, in mathematics?

Mr. Sublett: I was just average in mathematics at that time. I probably did better in physiology and anatomy, maybe humanities. I had a little problem with Spanish. I stopped taking that, because I didn't need it anyway.

Q: What year were you graduated in?

Mr. Sublett: I would have graduated in '42. I did not. I went a little better than three years. Then I worked. As a kid, I started out working odd jobs, and when I was in high school, the summer work was at the Buick dealership in Wilmette. I worked there as a part-time helper, simonizing and delivering cars and that sort of thing.* As a matter

---
*Simoniz was the trade name for a type of automobile polish; thus simonizing developed as a verb to describe the process of waxing and polishing cars.

Sublett #1 - 10

of fact, I went back to that particular job when I came out of the service.

I was also offered a job with my father-in-law.* I had gotten married when I was in the service, after I got my commission. He was an alderman in Evanston, and he was a member of the county board, and he wanted me to get into that. But I didn't want politics. It wasn't paying enough anyway. I had to get some money. I worked in the automobile business and did physical work instead of sitting down at a desk looking at papers and pushing pencils, listening to the political garbage, which is what I call it still.

Q: Why didn't you stay in school until graduation?

Mr. Sublett: I came out to go into the service. As I said, I was trying to get into the Air Force. At that time I think I weighed about 215 to 220, maybe, and I had to get down to 190 to get in the Air Force, so I did. But after I did that, there was no opening. I had turned 22 in March of that year. That was a few months after the bombing of Pearl Harbor. I was eligible for the draft but did not want to go in the Army. I love water; I've always loved water. I was a good swimmer and a fisherman, so I enlisted in the Navy.

―――――――――
*Mr. Sublett's father-in-law was Eugene Beck.

Sublett #1 - 11

Q: Had the general service ratings opened up to blacks at that point?

Mr. Sublett: When I enlisted, on 7 July 1942, the Navy just shortly before that had opened up other areas than cooks and bakers and steward's mates.*

Q: Did that make a difference for you in deciding to go into the Navy?

Mr. Sublett: I definitely wasn't going in to be a cook or a baker. I would have gone to the merchant marine probably or become a stevedore before I'd have gone in for that sort of thing. I wasn't qualified to be a cook or anything else like that. I didn't want to be one, and I definitely wanted to be a seaman. I enjoyed it.

Q: What do you remember about your experiences at boot camp at Great Lakes?

Mr. Sublett: At boot camp, I enlisted as an apprentice seaman. I had a good tour of duty in my entire hitch in the Navy, starting out from boot camp on up. We were in

---

*The change that permitted entry by black enlisted men into the general service ratings became effective in June 1942.

one of the earlier companies up at Great Lakes. That's where I did my boot camp--at Camp Robert Smalls.* I went through that in eight weeks.

Q: Did you have any trouble adjusting to the military discipline?

Mr. Sublett: None whatsoever. When I was 16, I went to Fort Riley, Kansas, for two weeks in the summer. It was called CMTC, Citizens Military Training Camp. I had some good military training there, including drilling, marksmanship with a rifle, and hiking. I've always been regimented and well-disciplined anyway, from the time I was a kid all the way up, so I had no trouble in that area. As a matter of fact, I became an apprentice CPO, one of the leaders in the company in boot camp.**

Q: Was that based on your experience at Fort Riley?

Mr. Sublett: Not experience, but my capabilities, actually. They didn't know that I had been at Fort Riley and it wouldn't have had any bearing on it anyway,

---

*Camp Robert Smalls was the site of recruit training for black sailors at the Naval Training Station, Great Lakes, Illinois. It was named for an escaped slave who captured the Confederate steamer Planter during the Civil War and turned her over to the U.S. Navy. He served as pilot of the Planter and later of the gunboat Keokuk.
**CPO--chief petty officer.

Sublett #1 - 13

probably.

Q: What capabilities were you singled out for?

Mr. Sublett: Leadership, I suppose. That could have come from football, could have come from track, or general education, or inherited from Mom or Dad. I don't know.

Q: Probably military bearing.

Mr. Sublett: Military bearing definitely would be involved.

Q: What were involved in your duties as a leader at boot camp?

Mr. Sublett: To assist in making inspections, certainly to assist some of the men who did not know about cleanliness and how to get clean. At that time they were drafted; some of those fellows came from places in the hills and didn't know what running water and good soap were. So in that area: drilling, general seamanship, and cleanliness. That's about it. I knew about knots and so forth from my Boy Scout experience.

Sublett #1 - 14

Q: You, I suppose, are one of the youngest members of the Golden Thirteen.

Mr. Sublett: I am, yes.*

Q: How did you compare in age with your peers at boot camp?

Mr. Sublett: There were some older than I, not particularly many. Generally I would say we were about the same age. I was probably a little bit younger. I was more educated than most of them, definitely. And that definitely had a bearing on my capabilities.

Q: What did the boot camp curriculum include?

Mr. Sublett: Learning basic knots, drilling. As a matter of fact, I called cadence when we drilled and marched. Some of the men didn't know their right from left. Some of the young men were illiterate.

Q: Were there remedial reading programs as part of boot camp?

---

*Both Frank Sublett and John Reagan were born 5 March 1920; all of the other men in the Golden Thirteen were born earlier.

Sublett #1 - 15

Mr. Sublett: There were remedial programs, yes. I didn't get involved in those. They had special setups for remedials. I didn't get involved in instructing until after I was in for a year or so and they sent me to a VD prevention school. And I did instruct on that, after I spent a couple of weeks back here at Great Lakes to learn how.

Q: Whom did you report to in your capacity as a recruit chief petty officer?

Mr. Sublett: At that time we called him company commander. He was a chief petty officer in the Navy, a chief that was over our boot camp company. The chiefs were responsible to the battalion commander and the battalion consisted of a bunch of boot camp companies.

Q: How many men were in your company, would you guess?

Mr. Sublett: At that time in boots, there must have been 150 or something. I hope I'm close on that. See, we slept in hammocks when I first went in.

Q: Did that take some getting used to?

Mr. Sublett: The first time it did. Every night somebody

hit the deck, because they were told to make the hammocks taut in the stays. A lot of fellows were afraid of falling on the deck, and they wanted to sleep with a sway in it because they thought it was more comfortable. Sure enough, they'd flip out of it. They'd have sore backs, they'd pee in the bed. Sleeping in that kind of position started the kidneys. That took some getting used to for some. That was more of a joke than anything else.

Q: How was the Navy chow?

Mr. Sublett: The Navy's chow was good. As a matter of fact, I didn't complain, not at all. A lot of fellows complained; they didn't want beans for breakfast on Saturday morning. That was a good meal for me.

Q: That was Navy tradition.

Mr. Sublett: That's right. Absolutely.

Q: What were the liberty opportunities for boot camp?

Mr. Sublett: There was no liberty while you're in boot camp. I recall that my folks used to come up. They lived here in Glencoe, so it was convenient for them to ride up and drive by outside the gate. We were close to one of the roads that goes by it, in our barracks. They'd come by and say "Hi," or something like that. But there was no liberty until after boot camp was finished. I've forgotten what the length of liberty was before we shipped out to service schools in various areas.

I went to Hampton, Virginia, after taking aptitude tests at boot camp to see what I was best qualified for.* My talent was in machinery, probably from having a background of working with the automobiles.

Q: Did that appeal to you?

Mr. Sublett: It did, sure. I liked it. I went to Hampton, Virginia, and studied at machinist's mate school. I finished successfully and graduated from that as a second class machinist's mate.

Q: Was that an integrated class?

Mr. Sublett: It was not. It was all black. As a matter of fact, both my boot training and secondary service school were all black. These were my first experiences with all black people, but no problem, none whatsoever. Some of the

---

*After the opening of the general service ratings to black enlisted men, many received their training at Naval Training School, Hampton, Virginia. The school was established on the grounds of Hampton Institute, a vocational college for black students.

Sublett #1 - 18

guys used to tease me about the way I talked, because they came from areas in the South, and I grew up here on the North Shore with a language or accent that was different from everyone else's. That didn't bother anybody or create any problems.

Q: Was there a good deal of camaraderie in these units you were in, both at Great Lakes and Hampton?

Mr. Sublett: Yes, there was, real good.

Q: I would think a spirit of patriotism, too.

Mr. Sublett: I think definitely that. Some didn't know why they were there, of course, those who were drafted, and didn't want to be there. There were some. Those were the ones that we had to help a lot to get into the thick of things, so to speak, or into the correct attitude, a positive attitude about the Navy and what they were there for. Even if you didn't want to be there, you're there, and make the best of it. That sort of thing.

Q: The future Admiral Gravely also attended machinist's

Sublett #1 - 19

mate school.* Did you cross paths with him then?

Mr. Sublett: No, I did not. I don't know where he attended it, as a matter of fact. Did he go through Great Lakes also?

Q: I thought he went to Hampton for his machinist's mate school.

Mr. Sublett: He might have, but not when I was there. I was in the first class that went through Hampton, Virginia, at machinist's school.

Q: That stands to reason, since the rating had just been opened up to blacks.

Mr. Sublett: Right. They had electrician's mate school, metalsmith, machinist's mate. All those below-deck ratings were at Hampton; service schools for the above-decks ratings were at Great Lakes: boatswain's mates and signalmen and that sort of thing.

Q: It must have been really a great satisfaction to put on those petty officer chevrons.

---
*In 1971 Samuel L. Gravely, Jr., became the first black naval officer selected for promotion to flag rank. He eventually retired as a vice admiral; he has been interviewed as part of the Naval Institue's oral history program.

Sublett #1 - 20

Mr. Sublett: It really was. When we started out, we had just one stripe for a seaman, and then after we completed boot camp, we had three on each cuff. After service school, I got the two chevrons for second class machinist's mate, and the insignia was a propeller. It was a real good feeling after completing that service schooling. Then after graduating from Hampton, Virginia, I was shipped up to East Boston in a machine shop, Pier One. Then I did machinist's work in there.

Q: Did you deal with repair work on ships?

Mr. Sublett: We worked on auxiliary pumps and propeller shafts and things like that. They didn't throw us right in. This was my first integrated navy assignment, in this machine shop. There were some much older white fellows in that outfit who were experienced machinists and probably came in the service after having been machinists in civilian life, so they were instructors, too. But I had menial jobs, I would say, to do as a machinist.

Q: Did they take an interest in training you and passing on their skills?

Mr. Sublett: They definitely did. One, in particular--I think his name was Bodine; he was our instructor. He was a

Sublett #1 - 21

boatswain's mate. Another fellow by the name of Doback; he was a very good machinist. I remember those two names because they were outstanding people in the field.

Q: Where did you live when you were there?

Mr. Sublett: We lived on the base, in a barracks.

Q: Was this at the shipyard?

Mr. Sublett: This was at East Boston Navy Base. It was called Pier One. No, it wasn't the Boston Navy Yard; it was far from there. It was on the Atlantic; Boston section base, it was called.

Q: Was there a floating dry dock there?

Mr. Sublett: No, there was not. There were no big ships, as a matter of fact.

Q: What sort of craft did you deal with?

Mr. Sublett: We dealt with the smaller craft. As a matter of fact, my next assignment was to go aboard one of those converted fishing boats.* Then I was on sonar duty,

---
*Mr. Sublett's records indicate that the craft was a converted fishing boat named the Queen of Peace (A-45).

Sublett #1 - 22

listening for submarines and that sort of thing. That was far from being a machinist.

Q: What memories do you have of that service?

Mr. Sublett: Just listening to the clang of buoy bells, and once in a while you'd hear a big ship go by. We tried to distinguish which sound was which. It was just in the Boston Bay area. We didn't get out to open sea in this little converted fishing boat. It was a precautionary measure, I guess, to see if any subs might slip through. I didn't stay on that too long. I went back to East Boston, to the machine shop on the base.

Q: Did you find that you enjoyed that work as a machinist's mate?

Mr. Sublett: I did. I liked it there. I liked it a lot. I probably learned a lot, because I did study at that time, too, and that's where I got my first class machinist's mate rating, at that base.

Q: Did you have people working for you?

Mr. Sublett: No, I didn't. I was just part of the crew at that time; I didn't have any leadership responsibilities.

Sublett #1 - 23

Q: How large a group were you in?

Mr. Sublett: I don't recall that now. There was a double-decker barracks there. We had the pool tables and we had the mess hall and all the facilities that we needed. It was a big pier, because we used to get up early every day and go out for calisthenics before morning chow. I don't recall how many people were involved there--maybe 150.

Q: How was the work assigned?

Mr. Sublett: I don't remember that. I was just verbally told what I would be doing today. Being a second class machinist's mate, you wouldn't be qualified to take any top assignments anyway; you would more or less still be an apprentice type, actually. To do the practical work, we learned the basics in the classroom work during the school, of course, and we did have a machine shop there at school, too, making various things. We weren't qualified to do big assignments on our own.

Q: Then I see you went to fuel injection school also.

Mr. Sublett: While I was in Boston, that's right, I went up to Springfield, Massachusetts, to Bosch Fuel Injection School for one week. It was kind of a supplementary school

Sublett #1 - 24

involving small engines, auxiliary engines.

Q: Diesels, I would think.

Mr. Sublett: Diesels. Right. So we didn't get involved with huge boilers and turbine type engines. We learned the basic function of them, but most of my work was with smaller engines, auxiliaries.

Q: But you were expanding your capability as a machinist's mate.

Mr. Sublett: Right. Definitely.

Q: Essentially, you spent that whole year of 1943 as a machinist's mate.

Mr. Sublett: I really did, yes, and I liked it a lot. That was all I did from Hampton after school through '43.

Q: How did you find out you were going to officer training?

Mr. Sublett: I didn't find out until I got there. I was told to lash my gear in seagoing fashion, and I was shipping out.* I learned one day, and then I was out the next day. I was going to Great Lakes, my orders said. I did not know why I was going to Great Lakes.

One of the men involved in our group was Phillip Barnes, whose sister worked in Washington in the Navy Department.** After we had been there for a couple of days, she told him there would be some men in the Navy who were going to be picked to go to officers' training school. We found out then why we were there. There were 16 of us at that time.

Q: Did that come as a considerable surprise?

Mr. Sublett: It was to me. I mean, all of a sudden to get involved in something this glamorous. Wow! I knew of the V-12 programs over at Northwestern and various other colleges, Purdue and so forth, and I think there was a V-7 program also.*** They did not take any black kids, none at all, in the naval ROTC.**** That's why we went to Great Lakes, because it was a special school set up just for us.

---
*Seagoing fashion called for the lashing of an individual's hammock around his seabag, which was filled with his uniforms and other gear.
**Phillip George Barnes was a member of the Golden Thirteen. He died before he could be interviewed for the Naval Institute's oral history program.
***The V-12 and V-7 programs trained college men as Naval Reserve surface officers; the V-5 program was for Naval Reserve aviators.
****ROTC--Reserve Officer Training Corps.

Sublett #1 - 26

Q: Did you find out how you happened to be one of the ones chosen?

Mr. Sublett: I'm certain that Commander Downes, who was commanding officer down at Hampton, Virginia, submitted my name as a candidate.*

Q: Had you had a close relationship with him?

Mr. Sublett: I had been a battalion commander during the time I was in service school for machinist's mate training. As an assistant to the commissioned officers, I'm sure that my commanding officer, Downes, was impressed by my attitude and my know-how, and he recommended me.

He gave me one heck of a good compliment one day. I've forgotten exactly how he put it, but he told me that he wished one thing in life, and that would be that his son Hall would grow up to be as fine a gentleman as I. I thought that was the greatest thing I'd ever heard. It really was. He was a very fine gentleman. He contacted my mother personally and told her of my progress in the machinist's mate school, and he kept tabs on everyone else in the company. He knew our names, he knew where we were

---

*Commander Edwin H. Downes, USNR, was a Naval Academy graduate who had resigned his commission, worked in the field of education, and then been recalled to active service for World War II. He was officer in charge of the Naval Training School at Hampton, Virginia.

Sublett #1 - 27

from, our background. He was a fabulous guy. He's the one, I'm sure, who recommended me for officer training, because I spent more time there than anywhere else.

Q: What sort of indoctrination did you get when you arrived at Great Lakes for officers' school? Was John Dille in it from the beginning?

Mr. Sublett: No, I don't remember how Dille was.* Like I said, I spent less time at Great Lakes than a lot of other guys, like White and Barnes and some of the others.** They knew Dille and Commander Armstrong and some of the others, because they were stationed there even after our class.*** But I don't know what the first part of our program was in the indoctrination. As far as I can recall, they told us why we were there, what we were up against, what we had to do to achieve our aims, and bang, there we were--books and studies.

Q: What sort of things did you study? What was the

---
*Lieutenant (junior grade) John F. Dille, Jr., USNR, was a battalion commander at Camp Robert Smalls. He has been interviewed as part of the Naval Institute's oral history program because of his close relationship with the Golden Thirteen.
**William Sylvester White and Samuel Edward Barnes were two members of the Golden Thirteen who remained on active duty at Great Lakes after being commissioned. The oral histories of both are in the Naval Institute collection.
***Commander Daniel W. Armstrong, USNR, was officer in charge of Camp Robert Smalls.

Sublett #1 - 28

curriculum?

Mr. Sublett: Navigation, seamanship, gunnery, small weapons, 20-millimeter and 40-millimeter guns. We still had to go through the obstacle course for fitness, that sort of thing, Navy Regulations. I've forgotten the other things.

Q: Who were the instructors?

Mr. Sublett: I don't recall those either. They were mostly junior officers. I think the officers were Annapolis graduates who were unqualified for sea duty.

Q: Did you get graded on your classroom work?

Mr. Sublett: We were graded, but I don't recall having seen any of the grades until afterward--at the completion of our studies.

Q: Was there a sense of competition among the officer candidates?

Mr. Sublett: No. There was a sense of camaraderie, very close, because we stayed in the same barracks, we studied together, and some of the men had not had sea duty at all. What little sea duty I had, I learned a lot, and some of the others had, too. One or two fellows had been aboard a tug or some small converted yacht or something like that. Where one man might be a little weak in knots or seamanship or something, the other was strong, and we just collaborated all of our efforts and got it. Navigation was a toughie--sextants and that sort of thing, and a lot of people hadn't seen one before and didn't know what they were. It was more or less a full cooperative effort on everybody's part. The men in our group had the capacity and ability to grasp the information. But not having experienced it, of course, why then it was all new. We just worked together.

Q: The Navy had a great pool to draw on, so it could pick people likely to succeed.

Mr. Sublett: Yes. That's exactly why they selected us, I'm sure. There were a lot they could have picked from, so they really narrowed it down. I've forgotten what they started out with, 600 or something like that, and narrowed it down to--I think there were 16 of us.

Q: You wound up with 13.

Sublett #1 - 30

Mr. Sublett: We wound up with 13 in the original group.

Q: Why did the other three not make it?

Mr. Sublett: That I'll never know, I suppose. I have no idea why they did not make it. You see, we were screened by the FBI, our local police stations, all the schools that we had attended, and I don't know who else. This is before we were picked.

Q: That's where your clean living paid off.

Mr. Sublett: Indeed. I heard of one small insignificant incident that caused one of the men to be dropped out of the program. I don't know for sure what it was. Not having talked with him directly, I wouldn't know.

Q: At the Naval Academy, for example, there's a great attention on grades and who stands where. I take it you didn't have that kind of emphasis.

Mr. Sublett: We did not. This was all new, and they didn't expect us to make it anyway, as far as that was concerned.

Q: What makes you say that?

Sublett #1 - 31

Mr. Sublett: This was a new experience, to have all these black people in the Navy in the first place, other than being mess cooks and that sort of thing. So they were taking a risk. Somebody was going to have problems if we didn't make it, whoever recommended the program. It was a pressure thing on all sides, I'm sure.

Q: Did you feel pressured?

Mr. Sublett: I didn't, no. I played football and was in track, involved with people and in social life, too. I was open-minded all the way through life and still am. It didn't give me any pressure. We were supposed to be intelligent people.

Q: It seems there was the expectation you would make it, or at least an effort to make it work.

Mr. Sublett: It was something new. Certainly we were qualified in some respects. I'm sure they thought that, or they wouldn't have recommended us. But still, the higher-ups might have been saying, "Oh, boy, look what we've got here. What are we going to do with them?" That sort of thing. They wondered what they were going to do with us after we got our commissions, anyway. We had menial jobs.

Sublett #1 - 32

That's why we had to be open-minded, because they didn't know where to put us.

Q: But picking good men, though, I think it was a good-faith effort.

Mr. Sublett: In that respect, yes. They wouldn't have put themselves out under the boom too readily if they hadn't expected some of us to make some good effort and come out of it with a positive attitude.

Q: I can imagine a scenario in which run-of-the-mill people were picked, they failed, and the Navy said, "Look, we've tried Negro officers, but it didn't work." That wasn't the way it happened.

Mr. Sublett: Right. That is true; it did not happen that way.

Q: I'd like to run through the names of your fellow officer candidates and just see what individual memories you have of them.

Mr. Sublett: That's going to be tough, because we hadn't associated with each other since the Navy days until 1977. I hadn't talked with any one of them, hadn't seen any one

Sublett #1 - 33

of them, although two of them live in Chicago, White and Arbor.* But I had not communicated with any of them.

Q: I'm interested in what you remember of them from 1944. What about Arbor? What kind of a guy do you remember him as?

Mr. Sublett: During our indoctrination, Arbor was kind of a relief valve, I think, one of them anyway. When we got into a puzzling problem, he'd come up with a joke or maybe a silly answer. I can remember him that way, and he still is that way.

Q: I talked to him on the telephone. He was Mr. Energetic, very loquacious.

Mr. Sublett: Yes, yes. He was well exposed to the public, too, having had a cleaning business and so forth, a pretty worldly man.

Q: How about Phillip Barnes?

Mr. Sublett: Phil Barnes I didn't know. I think Phil had been a teacher. I don't know too much about Phil. He was

---
*Jesse Walter Arbor is a member of the Golden Thirteen. His oral history is in the Naval Institute collection.

Sublett #1 - 34

pleasant, he laughed a lot. I don't remember anything particularly outstanding. I think he was more studious. He had not had any sea duty as an enlisted man. He was one of the weaker ones in the area of seamanship and that sort of stuff. He came through okay.

Q: Samuel Barnes.

Mr. Sublett: Sam Barnes was a well qualified educator. I'll say that. I don't remember too much more than that about Sam. He participated in several athletic programs.

Q: Dalton Baugh.*

Mr. Sublett: Dalton Baugh. The most I remember about Dalton is that he was from Pine Bluff, Arkansas. That was his big thing. He went to school down there. He was a good man, a good student, intelligent. I don't remember anything outstanding.

Q: George Cooper.**

Mr. Sublett: I had known Cooper, I think, at Hampton,

---
*Dalton Louis Baugh was a member of the Golden Thirteen. He died before he could be interviewed by the Naval Institute's oral history program.
**George Cooper is a member of the Golden Thirteen. His oral history is in the Naval Instiute collection.

Sublett #1 - 35

Virginia, before we became commissioned officers. He was a knowledgeable educator. That's all I can say about George.

Q: Reginald Goodwin.*

Mr. Sublett: Reggie was a Chicago man. I guess he was an attorney. I didn't know Goodie too well. He was a very staid person.

Q: I got the impression from Justice White that Goodwin was sort of a liaison man with the higher-ups.

Mr. Sublett: I heard that same thing, but I don't know, because I didn't know Goodie that well.

Q: James Hair.**

Mr. Sublett: Oh, gee, I don't recall Hair too much. Just a regular guy, that's all I can say about Hair.

Q: Charles Lear.

Mr. Sublett: Lear was a good man, a good, strong guy. Of

---

*Reginald Ernest Goodwin was a member of the Golden Thirteen. He died before he could be interviewed for the Naval Institute's oral history program.
**James Edward Hair is a member of the Golden Thirteen. His oral history is in the Naval Institute collection.

Sublett #1 - 36

course, it turned out that he wasn't afterwards, though.*

Q: He was the only one commissioned as a chief warrant officer.

Mr. Sublett: He did get a commission as a chief warrant. There was one other who was studying to be a warrant officer, but he didn't make it--Alves.** I don't know what to say about Lear. He was from Keokuk, Iowa. He lived in Lake Forest afterwards, but I didn't know too much about Chuck at that time, during the school days.

Q: Mr. Dille suggested that he got commissioned as a warrant officer because he didn't have as much education as the rest of you.

Mr. Sublett: That was it, yes.

Q: Graham Martin.***

Mr. Sublett: I remember Graham because of football. He was an outstanding football player down at Indiana.

---
*Charles Byrd Lear was a member of the Golden Thirteen. He committed suicide shortly after World War II ended and he had been released from the naval service.
**A. Alves was one of three enlisted men who went all the way through the officer training with the Golden Thirteen but were not commissioned.
***Graham Edward Martin is a member of the Golden Thirteen. His oral history is in the Naval Institute collection.

Sublett #1 - 37

Q: So you certainly had that in common.

Mr. Sublett: I knew that, yes, and a hell of a teacher.

Q: Both Big Ten men.

Mr. Sublett: Yes. He had been a teacher also. He was a good man. We served a lot together after our commissioning in Eniwetok. We were out in San Francisco together, served aboard two different craft, a yard oiler and a patrol craft. We were in a logistics support company together out in Eniwetok.

Q: Did you get a chance for sports or exercise during the training period as officers?

Mr. Sublett: Yes, but I've forgotten all what it was. I'm sure we did, because we did have to go through the obstacle course, I remember that, as a beginning, to qualify. I've forgotten what other programs we were involved in. I don't know whether it was regimented or whether we were on our own, but certainly we had some sort of a program to do besides study all the time.

Sublett #1 - 38

Q: You would have a great deal of togetherness, this group of just 16 separated from everybody else.

Mr. Sublett: Right. I don't know what our physical program was, because some of the fellows were not physically oriented; several of us had played football. Like Reagan played football and Martin and myself and Arbor.* I've forgotten, but we did have some recreational activities.

Q: Dennis Nelson.**

Mr. Sublett: He had been a recruiter. I don't think he went through boots. He was a first class petty officer as a recruiter down in Nashville, Tennessee, or something like that. He was the mouth of the group--good and bad. Guys used to get pretty sore at him, because he'd come up with the darnedest things, but we all loved him.

Q: What sorts of things would he come up with?

Mr. Sublett: Oh, gee, I don't know now. He was stationed, after our commissioning, at Great Lakes, and I guess he had

---
*John Walter Reagan is a member of the Golden Thirteen. His oral history is in the Naval Institute's collection.
**Dennis Denmark Nelson II was a member of the Golden Thirteen. He died before he could be interviewed for the Naval Institute's oral history program.

Sublett #1 - 39

problems with Commander Armstrong about wearing different types of uniforms that he wanted. He wanted the glamour of it. The glamour boy and that sort of thing, but I don't recall exactly what type of things he would instigate or cause somebody to say, "Oh, shut up, Nelson," or something like that. But nothing serious.

Q: Justice White remembers him as a very proud man.

Mr. Sublett: He was proud. He died proud. He loved the Navy, he really did.

Q: I've seen the 1977 reunion picture. He, alone among the group, was wearing a uniform.

Mr. Sublett: Yes. He stayed in. He shipped over to regular Navy and became a lieutenant commander. We were all Navy Reserve, and he shipped over to the regular Navy. He loved it. As a matter of fact, I think one or two of his sons served in the Navy also.

Q: He was at Eniwetok also, wasn't he?

Mr. Sublett: He was. He was there with me and Martin. We were at the same base, Logistic Support Company 515. He was our personnel officer at that time. Lieutenant Reed

Sublett #1 - 40

was our commanding officer, and I was the executive officer, and I was also supply.* Nelson was personnel, Martin was recreational, and I don't know what other capacity he served out there. We had a nice group over there.

Q: You mentioned that Reagan was a football player. What else do you recall about him?

Mr. Sublett: He was my best man at my wedding. He was at Hampton the same time I was during service school, because he was studying to be an electrician's mate. I knew him a little better than I knew anybody else, actually.

Q: So he was probably your best friend?

Mr. Sublett: He was my best friend.

Q: Judge White--any recollections of him?

Mr. Sublett: I didn't know anything about Syl until we met there at the school. I didn't know him at all, just as a lot of the others, like Goodie and Baugh and the Barneses. I didn't know any of them. I had gone through boot camp ahead of all of them.

---
*Lieutenant (junior grade) George W. Reed, USNR.

Q: He was among the best educated of the group.

Mr. Sublett: He went to the University of Chicago and had his degrees and had practiced law.

Q: Did that count for anything, or were you all essentially equal in the training scheme?

Mr. Sublett: We were all the same. White went to the University of Chicago, one of your elite schools. Somebody else might have gone to a southern school, and somebody went to Howard University, which is a black college. You couldn't evaluate the differences in those. I don't know how they did, as a matter of fact.

Q: Another who didn't make it through was Mummy Williams.* What do you recall of him?

Mr. Sublett: I knew Mummy at Great Lakes during the indoctrination period, but I don't know why he did not make it. I have no idea. He and Sylvester White were close, and they knew each other before the Navy, I think.

---

*Lewis Reginald Williams was one of the three enlisted men who went through officer training with the Golden Thirteen but was not commissioned. He has been interviewed as part of the Naval Institute's oral history program.

Sublett #1 - 42

Q: Yes. Williams was the one who got him in.

Mr. Sublett: Yes, he did. But I don't know what happened to Mummy, why he didn't make it.

Q: You mentioned the name of Alves also.

Mr. Sublett: Alves was from out East--I've forgotten now where. But he had been in the merchant marine prior to the Navy, and I don't know why he didn't make it. I don't know where he went to school either.

Q: There must have been one other to make a total of 16.

Mr. Sublett: His name was Pinkney; he was from Atlanta.* He was washed out; why, I don't know.

Q: Did some leave before the completion of the full course?

Mr. Sublett: No. The course was completed by everyone. Then they made the selection after the course's completion.

Q: You've mentioned the academic curriculum. There's also the part about becoming an officer and a gentleman. Was

---
*J. B. Pinkney.

Sublett #1 - 43

that Dille's role?

Mr. Sublett: No. With me personally, I don't recall what Dille's part was. I knew he was very effective with some, like Barnes and the people that were at Great Lakes. See, I was down in Virginia for service school. These other fellows--like Arbor, Barnes, White, Goodie, and Nelson-- were all at Great Lakes. That's how they were involved so much with Dille.

We studied like hell. We had to study hard. I guess you know we had a 3.89 average, which was pretty good, I guess.

Q: Yes.

Mr. Sublett: At that time, it was pretty good. Like I say, though, some were weak in some areas and some strong, so we got it together. Naval history was one of the toughies.

Q: Was there indoctrination in the fact that you're going to face some obstacles and possibly resentment once you get out and get commissioned?

Mr. Sublett: No, there wasn't any thought about that that

Sublett #1 - 44

I recall. I'm sure we didn't know who was going to make it, and that was a little far ahead to predict or anticipate. I wouldn't begin to anticipate something like that anyway. You face it if you make it.

Q: And take it from there.

Mr. Sublett: That's right. One day at a time in that case. I was never involved in any maltreatmet, I should say. I don't know of any disrespect. I know I didn't have the attitude that if they didn't salute me, that I was going to put somebody on report or anything like that. Nelson probably put people on report for not saluting up at Great Lakes. After all, there are several ways to look at it. You are wearing the uniform. A sailor's not saluting you personally or not saluting you. He may not salute you because of personal reasons; you're black. On the other hand, he's disrespecting the uniform by not saluting the uniform. There are all kinds of ways to pick that apart.

Q: So you were still using your "live-and-let-live" philosophy.

Mr. Sublett: Exactly right. Like I had the attitude, "If I go to sea and don't get back, okay. It's not my time to come back," or whatever. I wanted to go in and do what I

Sublett #1 - 45

could well and take it from there.

Q: Was there a special ceremony connected with the graduation?

Mr. Sublett: Nothing. We had no graduation ceremonies whatsoever. We were probably the only group of officers that ever received a commission that never had a graduation exercise of any sort.

Q: Were you bothered by that?

Mr. Sublett: No. I've forgotten how they presented our commissions now. However they did it, it was okay. I got it, got the uniform and that sort of thing, and I was qualified to do the next assignment. After that, I was shipped back down to Virginia.

Q: You were gathered for a group picture. So that was probably the most formal thing connected with your graduation.

Mr. Sublett: That was it. They put our picture in _Life_ magazine and several other publications.* Something new. Look at this. The country was due to see what was going

---

*"First Negro Ensigns," _Life_, 24 April 1944, page 44.

on.

Q: Did you feel like a celebrity?

Mr. Sublett: No, gee whiz. Probably I had the same attitude as when I went up to get my diploma in high school and shook the principal's hand or something like that, or when I went to get an award for my letter in high school sports.

I suppose that it's only lately that I've realized what we went through and how valuable it was. It is history. I hear the kids next door say, "I see you in our history book," or something like that. It didn't faze me. My kids have never told me that. Whether they saw it or not, I don't know. They hear it from other kids, maybe. I've just realized lately, since we've had our first reunion and thereafter, that this is something. There's been a lot of to-do made over us, so it is a historical thing. I'm proud to have been a part of it, but I'm not a flag-waver in that sort of situation.

Q: So that sense of pride is more in retrospect than it was at the time?

Mr. Sublett: Yes. Right. Exactly. I was in the Navy, and I wanted to be, and I was going to do what I had to do

Sublett #1 - 47

to make the best of it. I'm sure I kept that attitude all the way through.

Q: Did you have any choice at all where you would go once you were commissioned?

Mr. Sublett: No, none at all. I know that Commander Downes wanted Reagan and me back down in Virginia, so we were both assigned back there. I had a company of men, 250 of them, I guess, and I was in charge of them. It was similar to the group I had been a part of when I first went down there for service school.

Q: What were these 250 men there for?

Mr. Sublett: They were coming to the various service schools down there.

Q: Were they all black?

Mr. Sublett: They were all black, yes. I had a company, Reagan had a company. I instructed in small boat handling, seamanship, military bearing, and that sort of thing. I executed the duties of a commanding officer, actually.

Q: You probably also felt a sense of personal loyalty to

Sublett #1 - 48

Downes, so you were glad to go back.

Mr. Sublett: Right. I was happy to do what I could to be impressive, that he had made a good choice in that way, and so did the other officers that were there at that time also.

Q: Did you have a desire to go on board ship?

Mr. Sublett: I wanted to, yes. After leaving Hampton, Virginia, I went to the 12th Naval District--Treasure Island. That's when I was put aboard <u>YP-131</u>, which was a patrol craft. It was a converted yacht. That's why I stated earlier that I feel they didn't know exactly what to do with this group of black officers who were qualified to be deck officers. Martin, I think, was aboard with me on that one, or we alternated, because Martin played football over in San Francisco. He'd be on duty and I'd be off. Then I'd have the duty and he would be off. We'd change watches sometimes so that he could go play football--under an assumed name.

Q: Was this semi-pro ball?

Mr. Sublett: Yes. They used to play the El Toro Marines. I've forgotten the name of his team he used to play with.

Sublett #1 - 49

Q: Why under an assumed name?

Mr. Sublett: I guess you weren't supposed to collect the money for playing on the outside. So he had to do it that way; he felt that was better. When we served on this patrol craft, the crew was all black on there. Among other things, we took a bunch of nurses out for a ride up and down the bay. What other things did we do there? I don't know. Nothing important. Nothing involving warfare or anything like that. We continued to study Navy Regs and took correspondence courses in school, and other courses, too. I've forgotten what they were.

Q: What was the role of the craft? Was it analogous to the one you had been on in Boston, just a last-ditch defense thing?

Mr. Sublett: No, it wasn't. It didn't have that kind of gear on it. We'd go out on dummy torpedo runs with the submarines, more or less to keep traffic out of the area so the submarines, like the _Silversides_ and others, could make dummy runs and fire torpedoes. An escort type thing, just bay patrol, that's all.

Q: San Francisco is not too tough a duty.

Sublett #1 - 50

Mr. Sublett: No, that's kind of nice. I enjoyed that. We tied up at Treasure Island. After that we went aboard a yard oiler, YO-106. Martin and I still served as alternates in this yard oiler for the port director at that time in San Francisco. Typically we went to an oil refinery, picked up oil, and went alongside battleships, aircraft carriers, cruisers, destroyers, and all sorts of ships to refuel them day and night. That was good duty; that wasn't bad at all. It was something meaningful to me, so I liked it.

Q: Did you also enjoy it because of your interests in boats and the water?

Mr. Sublett: Yes!

Q: The barriers had been falling for blacks in the Navy, but there was still that barrier against an integrated crew on board ship.

Mr. Sublett: The first little patrol craft that I was on in Boston, there were two of us on there as machinist's mates that were doing this sonar bit. There were three of them and two of us, and I don't know whether we were on the same time or not. It was small.

Sublett #1 - 51

Q: Surely not shipboard duty.

Mr. Sublett: Not a ship, no. In the oiler, we had a couple of white kids on that one. They were capable, and they respected us. Everybody got along together as a crew; there was teamwork. That was the only mixed crew that I was involved with.

Q: Did you get any public attention at this point from your status as being one of the few black officers?

Mr. Sublett: No, I didn't. As a matter of fact, the people in California did not know that we were commissioned. Cooks and steward's mates wore uniforms similar to ours, with a cap and so forth. A lot of people didn't know the difference between a steward's mate and an ensign. They had not been indoctrinated on it. There was no recognition. There were some who knew and accepted it and praised and that sort of thing, but nothing big. They'd look, a lot of them, but most of them, I would say, were proud to see us--white and black. They were respectful. I didn't have any problems as some of the others did, but I didn't look for any.

Q: In early 1945, you mentioned you came back to Great

Sublett #1 - 52

Lakes for instruction on VD training. How did that come about?

Mr. Sublett: I figure they didn't have anything else for us to do. It must have been for future use.

Q: Did you actually get involved in training people then in VD prevention?

Mr. Sublett: Not a full length. Maybe a lecture or two, something like that, in the category of cleanliness, that sort of thing, for the new arrivals in the Navy, and some of those who were careless. It was a precautionary measure, and we gave instruction.

Q: From that, you went out to the Pacific. What was your status then? Did you have any choice in where you would go at that point?

Mr. Sublett: No, I had no choice, none at all. I went aboard a naval transport on 18 July 1945 to Pearl Harbor, the 14th Naval District.* One other officer was with me. We waited there for an assignment. Actually, it was an officers' pool at that time. I was probably there for several days or a week. Then I went to NOB Eniwetok in the

---
*Mr. Sublett's orders were to Naval Barracks, Manana, Oahu, Territory of Hawaii, for temporary duty.

Sublett #1 - 53

Marshall Islands.*

Q: Not as enjoyable as San Francisco.

Mr. Sublett: No, it wasn't, but, you know, it was good duty, actually. Beautiful water, go swimming every day. The water was so clear that in 20 feet of water, you could see the bottom, just as if it was right here. Looking for shells and that sort of thing. Unloading supplies from ships was the main duty of this outfit; occasionally we loaded. Of course, we had to get set up with conversion machines and recreational facilities, inspection, and that sort of thing. We did everything to set up a camp, so to speak.

Q: So you were in charge of a stevedore gang?

Mr. Sublett: That type of thing, right. Yes. Our guys had to do that. We had a lot of recreational time, of course.

Q: You mentioned conversion machines. What were they?

Mr. Sublett: Water. Salt water to fresh water.

---
*NOB--Naval Operating Base.

Sublett #1 - 54

Q: Was there an established base there when you got there?

Mr. Sublett: I think we set it up, if I remember right. Then we had to stand guard duty at the hospital ship out there, a Japanese hospital ship, prisoners out there, wounded, and whatnot. We had that type of duty. We were making preparations collectively for the invasion of Japan. There was a huge setup at Eniwetok for the gathering of all types of ships and weaponry for the invasion of Japan. We were quite busy there in that area.

Q: Did you work with the Seabees in building the base?

Mr. Sublett: The Seabees had laid the airstrip. The island was small. It was about three miles long, or something like that and maybe a half mile wide, or a little better maybe. The Seabees did the airstrip and that type of labor.

Q: The island is small, but the lagoon is very large.

Mr. Sublett: The lagoon was beautiful and large, yes, held a lot of ships. One of the best lagoons. I couldn't understand why they'd ever blast that thing away. I think it was one of the most useful things that they would ever

Sublett #1 - 55

acquire.

Q: It must have been an impressive-looking gathering of ships there.

Mr. Sublett: It was. It was absolutely massive. We were quite shocked when the word came that Japan had been bombed.* We were happy, too, of course, that we didn't have to go and lose a lot of lives over there, but we were getting ready.

Q: What was the mood on the island when the war ended?

Mr. Sublett: It was a happy day, a real happy day.

Q: Did you feel a sense of relief?

Mr. Sublett: I'm sure I did, but I don't know how seriously I felt about it or, "What do I do next?" or what attitude I really had about it.

Q: You hadn't been exposed to the danger that a lot of people had.

---
*U.S. Army Air Forces B-29 bombers dropped atomic bombs on 6 August and 9 August 1945. The Japanese ceased hostilities on 15 August.

Sublett #1 - 56

Mr. Sublett: No, that's right. I was fortunate in some respects, and yet I suppose I did my share. On the other hand, I helped to train some who did get involved with it, I know.

Q: And you really didn't have the opportunity to do more.

Mr. Sublett: No, I did not. I don't know if they expected us to. I'm sure there were none of our group who were actually involved in combat.

I would have liked to have stayed in the Navy, actually, but I had married after I had gotten my commission, and by that time I had a young son also. The war was over, and my mother-in-law advised me to come home. I could have gotten another half-stripe for staying longer.* I had enough points to get out. I would have liked to have made a longer career out of it, but she felt it was essential that I get home. So I responded.

Q: Where had you met your future wife?

Mr. Sublett: I met her when I was going to George Williams College, and she was going to the YMCA school down in Chicago. We were living in Evanston at that time. My

---
*Mr. Sublett was then a lieutenant (junior grade). He could have been promoted to the rank of lieutenant had he remained on active duty.

mother had moved to Evanston while I was in college at Wisconsin. This young lady lived in Evanston with her family.* Her father was an alderman. While she was at the YMCA school, I met her commuting back and forth to school. We dated. Then, when I went in the Navy, we were still together and were dating, and we got married 18 March 1944, right after my commissioning. I took her on some of my assignments, like to Virginia and to California. Before shipping out, my mother came out to California to say goodbye.

Q: I'm sure you were glad to get back from Eniwetok.

Mr. Sublett: Well, yes, I was, but I was expecting to go further, of course, from there.

After Eniwetok, I came back to Pearl Harbor 27 November on USS PC-813 and stayed about a week. Then I went back to San Diego 9 December on an aircraft carrier, USS Card (CVE-11), and stayed there for a few days.

Q: You were a jaygee by that point.

Mr. Sublett: I was a jaygee at that time. I made promotion to jaygee on July 1, 1945. So I laid over in San Diego with another young man, Sidney M. Smith, who was a

---
*Mr. Sublett's wife's maiden name was Eugenia H. Beck.

warrant machinist. He was from Washington, D.C., and he shipped out also from Eniwetok back to the States. Then from San Diego back to Great Lakes to the separation center. In February of '46, I was terminated from active duty to inactive duty, assigned to the reserves for an indefinite period. I was appointed to a regular commission in the Naval Reserve 23 May 1946.

Q: Did you keep up with that at all?

Mr. Sublett: I did not. I was in inactive reserves. I was never called to do anything.

Q: Had you any notion of what you might have been assigned to, had you stayed in?

Mr. Sublett: No, I don't. I haven't the slightest idea.

Q: There was no negotiation with your wife's family?

Mr. Sublett: No, just, "Come home." I was sorry to hear it, because I wanted to stay. I liked the Navy. I had a good tour of duty all the way through, and I didn't want to terminate it, because I didn't know what was back here, whether I should go back to school, finish, and get a degree, or work. It turned out that I went to work to take care of my family.

Q: What sorts of jobs did you get into after you returned?

Mr. Sublett: I went in the automobile business, with a dealership. I've done body work, I've been a mechanic, I worked in every department, in parts and everything else. I was an assistant service writer. After being assistant service writer, I became a service manager. I did that for about 34 years. I think I was the first black service manager for a GM dealership in the Chicago metropolitan area. I had a good experience there, real good.

After I had enough of that, I terminated at the end of '79, and then I got into the modeling business because of a young man who used to live across the street from me. He had been a model. He said, "Frank, you ought to be tired of getting up at 5:30 every morning, going to that place up there, listening to people scream about their cars. Why don't you give me a picture and let's go down to see my agent." So I did, and here I am. They don't use people like me every day, but the industry is not flooded with older models, so it worked out very nicely. I only signed up with the one agent. You don't make a heck of a lot of money on it, but it's fun. It's a lot of fun. When you do work, it's good pay, of course, but you don't get enough jobs.

Q: What sorts of jobs have you had?

Mr. Sublett: I've done work in industrial films. I've been a judge, I've been a doctor, I've been a pharmacist, I've done cover flyers for automobiles, a cover for a telephone company book. I've done commercials. The biggest was, I was Mayor Washington of Chicago walking away from the camera in a TV commercial for radio station WLAK; that ran for about a year or so.* That was in '84. Others I've done for a bread company and Pillsbury. Most of my work has been in print advertisements and I've done a couple of small movie bits, too.

Q: What movies were you in?

Mr. Sublett: Industrial films, that's all. I was a salesman, judge, and an extra in a couple of movies.

Q: Which ones were those?

Mr. Sublett: They were for Motorola and Allstate Insurance Company. I've been in a couple of training films. It's been a lot of fun. I just don't get enough of it, that's all.

---
*Harold Washington, the first black mayor of Chicago, held that office from 1983 until his death in 1987.

Q: Do you ever have any regrets that you didn't finish your college?

Mr. Sublett: No, not really, because I had a good work attitude and a good business going for me in the automobile industry. It was interesting. It used to be great. The reason I'm out of it now is that it's changed. It's not as interesting as it used to be, because our domestic automobiles are not what they used to be. The Japanese and the German automobiles have just about taken over the industry. It's just not fun. The prices are up high and the quality is down.

Q: And more complaints, probably.

Mr. Sublett: Yes. Well, I got by without ulcers. Sometimes a customer would come to the service entrance. You know he's there for a reason, a problem with his automobile. He might, on top of that, have another problem at home or in his business. He might want to unleash that on you. But you just handle that properly and don't have to get ulcers.

Q: You've got the sort of personality that would make you

deal with that in a diplomatic way.

Mr. Sublett: That's exactly what it takes. Right. In some areas, I'm sure it would not work, but in this North Shore area, having lived here and knowing that these people expect good service, I was able to give it to them. Chicago is totally different. The guy may come into your shop with a long knife and shout, "Why isn't my car running?"

My response to complaints was, "I didn't build your car, you know, but I can fix it. That's why I'm here." I don't know how long I would have lasted in someplace like Chicago. Anyway, I knew what the people were there for--a problem. You have to respect that.

Q: You've had a fair amount of involvement with the Navy in recent years. Are there any highlights of that you recall?

Mr. Sublett: I've looked forward every year to our reunion, our mini conferences that we have. It's good to see the guys again since we've gotten back to know each other a little better and we communicate. It's interesting to grow old together and laugh, have a few drinks, whatever.

Sublett #1 - 63

Q: Does the Navy ask you to get involved in recruiting at all?

Mr. Sublett: We are definitely involved as a unit in recruiting. I get mail from internal affairs to keep updated with situations in the Navy Recruiting Command. As a matter of fact, the Navy Recruiting Command sponsors our get-together every year anyway. They also sponsored our return to the sea in '82, when we went aboard the USS Kidd, one of our newer combat ships, a beautiful piece of machinery, beautiful, absolutely wonderful.* I liked that.

Q: In the pictures I've seen, you all have big smiles, so I take it you enjoyed yourselves.

Mr. Sublett: We enjoyed that immensely. It was great.

In my situation, there's nothing I can do, as one, around here. This town has less than 10,000 people in it. What we are supposed to be stressing is to encourage blacks to get into the Navy, realize what advantages there are for them now, as compared to what it was when we went in, what's available for them now, so far as getting an

---

*From 13 to 15 April 1982, the nine surviving members of the Golden Thirteen held a reunion on board the guided missile destroyer Kidd (DDG-993) at sea in the Atlantic. See PH2 Drake White, "Golden 13 Together Again," All Hands, August 1982, pages 8-11.

education.

The price of an education in the civilian world today is unaffordable, and you can go to the service, particularly the Navy, get a good education, make a career of it. If you learn a trade in the Navy, you can come out later and, if you desire, go into business, the corporate world or whatever. Of course, we have to work with the recruiters in the Chicago area. In our case, there are three of us. But as a group, that's what we are responsible to the recruiting command for. That is our aim.

Q: Do you make public appearances?

Mr. Sublett: I don't. George Cooper has done extensive work in it. Dalton Baugh did. I think Arbor has picked up on that particular phase in the last year or so since he has retired from where he was working. I don't know whether Hair has done group work or not. Reagan has done some work in that area, too. I'm sure there are some youngsters that are qualified in Chicago, but I don't know how White and Arbor are doing about reaching them. I know Syl had opportunities associated with the juvenile system in the city. Then there are certain situations that won't accept juveniles who've had some sort of a misdemeanor, and you can understand why. The qualifications are pretty

Sublett #1 - 65

stiff. With the sophisticated Navy that we have now, you've got to have well-qualified people. It's not like passing ammunition anymore; it's know-how, computerized.

Q: That's a big selling point, too, that that training can be used in civilian life.

Mr. Sublett: Absolutely. Then, too, those who are qualified already, after graduating from college, they're going into the corporate world. You know, money. Big money. That's going to attract them. Once in a while, you get ahold of a youngster and get him started in it. Then to retain them is another thing. Retention is something else in our minorities. They get to captaincy or even commander, why, after 20 years, boom, goodbye. Well, what are the other youngsters going to do when they come up? Maybe you get up to lieutenant and they quit or put in their time, whatever it is, instead of staying and providing leadership for others as role models.

Q: That's a temptation for people of any race.

Mr. Sublett: Absolutely. Minorities are already down anyway, so we try to encourage them to get in. It's a toughie.

Sublett #1 - 66

Q: I notice that Captain Reason, who was President Carter's naval aide, became the first flag officer from the class of '65 at the Naval Academy, and obviously the first black flag officer from that class.*

Mr. Sublett: Right.

Q: So some are staying in.

Mr. Sublett: Yes, some are. And there will be a few more admirals along.

Q: It's almost a good sign now that when a black man does make admiral, it's not such news anymore.

Mr. Sublett: No, it's just a run-of-the-mill thing. Just do your thing, do your job, and you can get there. That's what our goal is, to tell these youngsters. Join the Navy, do something worthwhile, and you'll achieve the good things in life. That's all it amounts to--do it. Individually, I haven't done anything like that. I had a relative who was in the Navy, but he's out now, I'm sorry to say. Kicked him out, believe it or not. Good to a certain extent, but the bottle got him in trouble. They don't tolerate that anymore. He was in a big aircraft carrier.

---
*Rear Admiral Joseph P. Reason, USN.

Q: Do you have anything to say in the way of a summation, or are there any questions I haven't asked that you would like to answer?

Mr. Sublett: I wish I had more to tell you. Again, I can say that for any youngster who is thinking of a career or going to school and learning a trade or a livelihood, the Navy is the best. I certainly would like to see more of our young men get into it and learn to be good citizens, which is first. A lot of people are complaining about what they don't do for blacks and this sort of thing, but blacks have to do for themselves, too. The first thing I would suggest is to be a good citizen, no matter who you are. You can make it. Learn to discard all those unpleasantries that are available in anybody's life. I had a real good tour of duty, and I'd do it again. I would, definitely.

Q: That's the best testimony on the experience.

Mr. Sublett: I certainly would do it again.

Q: And as you've discovered from the attention that the Navy has paid to you in recent years, you did have a history-making role.

Sublett #1 - 68

Mr. Sublett: It was. We had a part in the history of the world. It has dawned upon me lately that it was a significant, outstanding achievement, and I'm happy to have been a part of it.

Q: It's for that reason that I'm especially grateful to you for taking a part in our program and recording this so it can be on the record for people far in the future to use as a resource.

Mr. Sublett: Forever, we hope, whatever that is. I certainly appreciate your time and your effort on it. It's been a very pleasant association and a chance to bring back memories. Some of them I probably left out, but I think I've covered the basics pretty well.

Q: Thank you very much.

Interview Number 2 with Mr. Frank E. Sublett, Jr.
Place: Mr. Sublett's home in Glencoe, Illinois
Date: Thursday, 21 July 1988
Interviewer: Paul Stillwell

Q: It's great to see you again today, Mr. Sublett. I enjoyed our last meeting and look forward to filling in even more information this time.

One thing that I think you told me last time when the tape recording wasn't running was something of your own racial background, that there was a white ancestor in the immediate past.

Mr. Sublett: Yes. My mother's father was a Scotch-Irish gentleman. I didn't know him well, so that's all I can tell you about him. My mother is a mixture of Scotch-Irish and Negro, and there might be some Indian also--Cherokee.

Q: Was race something that was discussed much in your home when you were growing up?

Mr. Sublett: Race was never discussed in my home. Not at all. I was never race-conscious in any way. I grew up in this area as a child and through my high school years. We had a real nice association--we, meaning blacks, whites. I remember the Jewish, the Italians, Irish, and--in those

Sublett #2 - 70

days--Negroes.

Q: You were telling me you went to your high school reunion recently, the 50th anniversary. What was the reaction there?

Mr. Sublett: The reaction there was very, very congenial. It was much like the days when we were growing up and going through high school. There was no difference in attitudes about race. Race was never mentioned in those days, nor was it during the reunion, except for the fact that I told them I went to the officers' candidate school in the Navy and it was set up specifically for blacks. That was something they were not familiar with and wondered why. And, of course, we know today why--public attitudes are much different.

Q: And you told me that they complimented you on your youthful appearance, as well.

Mr. Sublett: I was complimented several times on how young I looked, and how healthy I looked, and that I was the one who had changed least. They had told me that on our 44th reunion, and I heard a lot this time. I feel real good about that.

Sublett #2 - 71

Q: What sorts of extracurricular activities were you involved in in high school?

Mr. Sublett: In high school I was in athletics, of course. I played football. I was on the track team. On the track team I threw the discus, and I put the shot, and I ran on the relay team. In football I played end and did the place kicking, kicking off and points after touchdown.

During the study hours, I was a study hall supervisor. I was a member of the chorus in my freshman and sophomore years.

Q: Did you win any honors as football player?

Mr. Sublett: I won honors each year that I played football and each year in track. All four years.

Q: What sorts of things?

Mr. Sublett: In your freshman year you got numerals, meaning the year that you graduate. In your sophomore year you got a certificate, meaning you duplicated your honor. In my junior and senior years, I received a school letter each year for football and track.

Q: Was there any coverage of black history in your school

Sublett #2 - 72

courses?

Mr. Sublett: No, there was not. Our school courses were arithmetic or mathematics, history, English, political science, chemistry, biology, and that sort. No studies regarding race or origin or anything like that.

Q: How much awareness at the time did you have of the racial climate in the South and other parts of the country?

Mr. Sublett: I had relatives down in Tennessee, but I was never aware of any difficulties they faced. I understand now that some lived under suppression, but there wasn't much talk about it. It was their way of life. Any time I visited in Tennessee there was good feeling between whites and blacks, as far as I could see. And they spoke to each other respectfully and did business together. And so I wasn't aware of any problems that were there, if there were any.

Q: I think that both sides had grown up in a way of life such that discrimination was just taken for granted.

Mr. Sublett: That's right; that was the way they lived. So a "nigger" was a "nigger," and a white man was a white man, and they lived their different ways. One knew what

Sublett #2 - 73

one's place was as far as I could see and hear about it.

Q: Do you have any memories of that time when you lived in Tennessee, before you moved here?

Mr. Sublett: All I remember as a kid, I had a goat for a pet. And I had a dog, and I had a rabbit. And I remember my grandmother--my mother's mother--boiling clothes in a big black iron kettle out in her yard, where she used to do laundry, washing all the sheets and so forth. I helped her draw water from a pump to fill this big kettle. My mother has a picture of me when I was doing those little chores. That's all I remember, except for my dad used to go hunting for birds. And I don't remember anything else about it.

Q: What do you remember about your father as a role model?

Mr. Sublett: Not too much, really. My dad was busy, away from home when I was a youngster down in Tennessee. And here in Illinois he was making a living the best he knew how--chauffeur and that sort of thing. And then he went to work in a railroad as a porter, a redcap, and a waiter.

The only role model aspect that would positive--I heard a lot of people approach him and talk about how great he was as a football player. And I was proud of that and certainly wished I could have seen his prowess on the athletic field. I heard a number of people compliment him on that.

Q: I wonder if that guided you toward football.

Mr. Sublett: It might have helped some, but I think just the environment that I grew up in was the biggest contributor to that, because it was available here. We played in grade school: soccer, basketball, boxing, and after school, football. And we had everything available for us here, and I just think I did best in football and soccer.

My dad and my mother divorced in 1931. I was quite young, so he didn't really contribute a lot to my upbringing.

Q: Did you feel the absence of that kind of influence after he was gone?

Mr. Sublett: No, I really didn't, because I'd see him occasionally. He'd come by and visit with us. But I lived with my uncle and my aunt, and my mother still worked close by as a domestic. I had an uncle that was good to me in that I used to go hunting, fishing, and camping with him. We used to go up to Wisconsin, to the lakes, and stay for a week or so on vacation time. And that's how I learned gardening. We had a huge garden. And I learned all the chores of gardening and how to raise vegetables and fruits.

I had a lot of chores to do. Back in those days we had coal heat, and I used to help shovel coal into the coal bin in the basement, stoke the furnaces, and also keep the hot water heater going. He used to make home brew, as a matter of fact, and I was instrumental in capping the bottles.

Q: Was that after Prohibition ended?

Mr. Sublett: It might have been during Prohibition, because I was just a kid then--ten years old perhaps.

Q: That would have been before the end of it.* Sounds like a useful enterprise to have.

Mr. Sublett: It really was, I guess. As a matter of fact, I can remember a little neighbor boy and myself took a drink of some of the beer once. And I think it made us a little dizzy, because it was quite potent. We were reprimanded for it, and nothing serious. That was the last time. It's like trying your first cigar. Got sick, a little woozy, and forget it after that.

---
*Prohibition ended in 1933, when Mr. Sublett was 13 years old.

Sublett #2 - 76

Q: Sounds as if your uncle became something of a substitute father.

Mr. Sublett: Yes, definitely he could be looked upon as that, because he saw that I had the necessary things to do to become a good man. I was never a problem child. He taught me all the good things that I know.

I went to work with him in the mornings before school. This was when I was probably around 12, 13 years old. I became a busboy in a tearoom where he worked. He was a janitor there, and I went in and did odd jobs, cleaning garbage cans, stacking and washing dishes, and clearing tables. So that became an after-school job and also weekend work. Then along with my caddying at the country club, I was mowing lawns and that sort of thing. We had a large house just a couple of blocks away from here and a large plot for gardening. So I had plenty to do.

Q: It sounds as if you really got a lot of your values for life from him.

Mr. Sublett: I truly believe that, yes. He had been in the service. He was in the World War I. He had been gassed during the war and had some sort of infection from it. He had to go off to a veterans' hospital for treatment occasionally.

It was a good life, living with my uncle and aunt. My aunt was my father's sister. My uncle had two brothers in Tennessee who owned a huge plot of land, and there is where they raised tobacco and farmed. And that's how I learned a lot more about the growth of food and raising chickens and that sort of thing. I used to raise chickens right here in Glencoe. I was quite proud of my Leghorns and Rhode Island Reds. During my grade school days, I kept little broods of chicks and raised them.

Q: You were too busy to be in any trouble.

Mr. Sublett: Absolutely. I was with the Boy Scouts in school and work at home. My uncle and aunt always knew where I was. If I wasn't at home in the yard, in the wintertime I'd be ice skating; in the summertime I'd be down at the beach, which was only a few blocks away; or I'd be over in the park playing baseball. They always knew where I was at all times.

Q: Please tell me more about your Boy Scout experiences.

Mr. Sublett: Oh, we used to go hiking. First of all, our sponsor was a wealthy man whose name was William Baehr. By the way, our Boy Scout troop was white and black. Mr.

Sublett #2 - 78

Baehr was white. He used to take us hiking; he'd take us to ball games at Cubs' Park and all the other niceties that Boy Scout troops do. We learned knot tying. And we went out camping; we knew how to cook out and sleep out overnight--all the regular things that young Boy Scouts learn. We had to know the scout manual thoroughly, so we could pass our tests and advance.

Q: You told me before that you believe that a person has an obligation to be a good citizen. I'm sure you learned some of that in Boy Scouts.

Mr. Sublett: That definitely contributed to my way of living, and it never left me. I still have that same attitude. It's the way to go.

Q: And, also, apparently from your father and your uncle, you got this love of the out-of-doors that was reinforced by the Scouts.

Mr. Sublett: Oh, indeed so. I love the out-of-doors. I like to go out and sleep under the stars.

Q: And you told me, also, that you got a position of leadership in the Scouts.

Sublett #2 - 79

Mr. Sublett: I went through tenderfoot, second class, first class, and became junior assistant scoutmaster. So I think that also helped my further education toward leadership. Mr. Baehr thought enough of my leadership qualities to give me that responsibility. And it relieved him of some of the burden and was helpful to everyone. I used to instruct on the knot tying for some of those who were a little slower, and I was also a bugler for the troop.

Q: But you had that sense of responsibility.

Mr. Sublett: Some of it, I suppose, was born in me. And the style of living that I grew up in, I'm grateful for. And the school system here, of course, is one of the best in the whole country. And the gym teachers, two of the science teachers, English teachers, and all the teachers that I had were contributors to good living and learning. A lot of it soaked in and stayed with me.

Q: What sort of black-white ratios were there in, say, the scouts and in school in those years?

Mr. Sublett: I think there were three blacks graduated in my grammar school class. I've forgotten what ratio that is to the whites, but there were four of us, or five who

Sublett #2 - 80

graduated from high school from a class of 539. In our recent reunion, three attended, including myself. But the ratio's been very small.

Q: You were never made to feel uncomfortable?

Mr. Sublett: Oh, my, no, absolutely not. I never did feel uncomfortable about being who I was.

Q: Did your mother sort of defer to your aunt and uncle in your upbringing?

Mr. Sublett: Not necessarily. She had her days away from work to be with us. She was a sister-in-law to my aunt, so they were like sisters, anyway. As a matter of fact, when Mother was not at work, why, she and my aunt used to go around together shopping and all sort of things like that. My aunt was in a catering business also, and so they had similar careers, because Mom was a cook at that time. In later years she became just a companion, but in earlier years she was a cook.

Q: I got the idea from what you said before that she didn't really impose all that much of a strict discipline.

Mr. Sublett: No, it wasn't really necessary to do so. We

Sublett #2 - 81

had house chores to do. I did, and my sister did. And I knew what I had to do. If I prolonged doing something, maybe I would be warned that I couldn't go and play football or baseball, or whatever game, or I couldn't go swimming until I finished my chores. But that was understandable to begin with, so there was never a problem.

You've heard of kids getting whippings or spanks or something like that. I think I had only about three or four in my life as a kid growing up. One time that I did get a spanking that I remember, I used to wear the Buster Brown collars when I was a youngster growing up. And I think I dashed some of my mother's perfume or toilet water on one of the collars and my dad gave me a switching, just because I got a spot on my Buster Brown collar. It didn't hurt anything, but it was the wrong thing to do.

Q: It sounds, also, as if you did not come into contact with people your own age who might have been a bad influence on you.

Mr. Sublett: No, I did not. There were probably a couple around here in this town at the time, but I wasn't aware of them at the time. Most of the girls and boys were clean livers, and there was just nothing to get into around here. I mean, everything that's available today, I'm sure was available then, like booze and maybe marijuana. I'm sure it was, but I didn't know about it; I didn't hear about it at all. I wasn't interested in smoking cigarettes or drinking. It just didn't appeal at all. And most of the kids around here had the same attitudes that I did. When we got to high school, of course, there were a lot of kids who could afford to buy a beer or cigarettes. They did it, but that didn't include me.

Q: Sounds like you lived a sheltered life.

Mr. Sublett: I probably did it to myself. Yes.

Q: Well, that's not bad.

Mr. Sublett: It seems to have been the thing to do in my case. Being overexposed to things that were unfavorable was just not my bag.

Q: You said before that your sister you considered more worldly than you. What did you mean by that?

Mr. Sublett: She wasn't interested in the same things I was. I mean, she liked to go to parties and dances. I went to school dances. She ran with older people.

I was large for my age at that time. And all the activities I did were with older boys in the area. For instance, we used to wrestle on the ground. When I was in grammar school, I had to box with the gym instructor, because I was bigger than the other kids. I just had fast growing years at once.

Q: How much of a social life did you have in high school?

Mr. Sublett: There were dances that were held down in Chicago that I used to go to. These were blacks. There was a group of prominent people in Chicago, social register types whose kids had debutante balls. And I'd gotten invitations to their dances and parties. And they were chaperoned. And they were nice, clean, no-problem parties. There was a party every month or so, but there weren't a lot of them. And occasionally that same group would come out here for a beach party. There were some young ladies who lived out here who were about my age, and they would have a beach party or a birthday party. And just a certain group of Chicago people were invited out. And they were the children of teachers, or postal workers, or doctors, and that sort of thing--the so-called better class.

Q: Certainly couldn't have been many black girls to date in your high school.

Mr. Sublett: No, there were not, but I wasn't interested

in dating then, anyway. There were only three girls my age. When I dated, it would always be group-type things. I didn't have any way to go back and forth to Chicago for dates.

Q: How much hunting and fishing did you do? Was that something you also enjoyed?

Mr. Sublett: Hunting and fishing--yes, I've always been a good shot. My first gun was a .22 rifle, single-shot, bolt-action. And I became quite an accomplished marksman with that. I gradually got into other areas of guns, and I collected them for a long time. I used to go dove hunting, pheasant hunting, duck hunting, and rabbit hunting, and so forth. I used to love it. Whenever the season opened, I'd be there. And for fishing it was darn convenient for me to walk from here to Lake Michigan. At that time the lake was receded. It isn't like it is now. There was 50 feet or more of beach, and a lot of piers along the lake shore.

I'd go down with a rod, or a pole and a line, and catch perch or shad or whatever, then come back home and clean them. If the fish weren't biting--the wind was blowing the wrong way or something like that--we'd go swimming in the lake and then come home. Beautiful, calm morning, nobody down there. You could go skinny-dipping.

Then I'd go fishing with my uncle up in Wisconsin. We

used to go to Lake Ivanhoe and also Lake Geneva and another little lake that was in southern Wisconsin. We'd catch sun perch and blue gills and bass. He'd always rent a rowboat, and we'd catch frogs at night for bait, and night crawlers and that sort of thing. We would go out and fish time after time; we had a lot of fun.

He used to go duck hunting when I was too small to go with him, down in southern Illinois. Some wealthy man that my aunt used to do catering work for owned some land down in southern Illinois, and he let my uncle go down there and shoot. One time I went duck hunting with him when I got to be old enough, and that was fun, sitting in the blind and shooting ducks.

I've always been an avid hunter. I've never gone big-game hunting, which I would like to do one day, but it's not safe anymore. Too many wild people out there. People should not have guns if they don't know how to value them.

Q: Well, all of this would tie in with your love of the outdoors and probably contribute to it.

Mr. Sublett: Definitely so. Absolutely. I mean, you go out and catch a batch of fish and bring them in and clean them right on that shore, and make a fire, and have your fresh fish.

And then we'd go hunting in the wintertime--rabbit

hunting. Go down to southern Illinois: Effingham, Jackson, around that area. Game would get pretty heavy if you didn't dress it a little bit. So you shoot rabbit and gut it right there, and slip it in your hunting jacket, and it would be lightweight. And the same with quail if you dress or take the innards out. There were a lot of foxes and crows around there. They were hanging around to eat all the entrails that you'd take out.

And, sure, I slept out in the car many a night after getting to a spot to hunt or fish, and to wait for daybreak, when we'd hit the water or hit the woods. It was great fun. We did a lot of squirrel hunting also.

Q: With all these other activities, when did you find time to study?

Mr. Sublett: Well, I had plenty of time to study after school. To tell you another thing, I was in bed by 9:00 o'clock. So I did my studying. There was no problem there. I didn't have to be coaxed to do it. And, of course, in high school we had study hall periods, and I didn't waste any time there. Being a study hall supervisor was not a real chore, because there were no disorderly people in there. Occasionally we had a little ruckus but nothing serious. We handled it.

Sublett #2 - 87

Q: Did you enjoy learning?

Mr. Sublett: I did, but I should have learned a lot more. I wish I had gone a little bit different route, though, in learning. I wish I had gone toward the business world instead of just a general course. I was headed for a B.A., and I should have been in a business field of some sort.

Q: Was it generally a college preparatory type course in your high school?

Mr. Sublett: Yes, that's right. It was, and much like it is today, I think--the basics, English and science and history and a foreign language, which hasn't been of any use now, but it was nice to know it, anyway.

Q: I have reflected back on the number of courses I took in high school and college that had absolutely no application after that.

Mr. Sublett: I wonder today why I had to read A Tale of Two Cities or something like that. I mean, understanding Darwin's theory is one thing, or something like that. Or one of Shakespeare's plays, okay, but not the whole book of them. Or Longfellow's poems--"Why did I need those?" I often thought.

Sublett #2 - 88

They evidently had some value.

Q: I think we learn about human qualities from fiction.

Mr. Sublett: Yes, there has to be something in there good for it. I mean, I can understand dissecting frogs or dogs and that sort of thing, which was to get a basic knowledge of how we live, and what functions our innards have, our organs. But a lot of things I thought of were useless.

Q: Did you have any teachers who particularly inspired you?

Mr. Sublett: On a couple of occasions I might have. They were both coaches. My football coach, as a matter of fact, told me at that time I was lazy. And it helped, because I graduated with an A in algebra. My track coach also advised me in that same area, that I could do better. I was doing all right, but they saw a potential to do even better. They would prod you a little bit, or make you feel like you should do more. In that area, yes.

Q: Do you think you would have benefited from more of that?

Mr. Sublett: I probably would. Later I probably would

have, but once you get to college, you don't get that type of attention. In high school, yes. I got it as much as there was. Everybody had an interest in your welfare and urged you to do better.

Q: Was there a fairly competitive atmosphere among the students scholastically?

Mr. Sublett: Not particularly. Everyone knew what the goals were. You could become a member of the dean's group, either the good one or the bad one. And they knew what the qualifications were to go to a particular college that they wanted--that the parents wanted them to go to, or what business they were going to enter. And in that way it was to their own advantage to really dig hard. But I think most of us went through just a period of learning how to study, and I probably went through too casually. I did well enough, but that shouldn't have been my goal. See, a lot of these kids came through high school, and came out of college, right into their daddies' businesses. And everybody didn't have that opportunity. They had to work hard and still don't have it.

Q: So you probably didn't have the advantage of a specific goal to focus on.

Mr. Sublett: I really didn't. I mean, after all, my dad was doing something that was menial. He and my uncle were living good, clean lives and doing work to survive, but there was no promise of a position in life or in business. And at that time many blacks were thinking about becoming teachers, doctors, or something like that, and I wasn't. I didn't know what to aim for, so that's why I just took a general course.

Q: Were there counselors at the school to give you that kind of steering?

Mr. Sublett: There were counselors for going to colleges. I went to the University of Wisconsin because of a counselor, as a matter of fact. I went because I played football. I did well in football in high school. And the alumni gentleman, who used to live a few blocks away from here, aided me in getting a job for my board and for my room at Wisconsin.

Q: What kind of a job did you have?

Mr. Sublett: I worked in the Phi Delta Theta house. I helped serve meals a couple of times a day. And so that took care of all my food.

I had another job with the NYA or some assistance

program for needy students.* And I helped a gentleman with his thesis. I used to type for him. I used to read for him. He was partially blind. And that's how I earned enough money for my room.

Q: How about the tuition?

Mr. Sublett: I paid for most of my tuition, because I had saved money for that. And, of course, working with the program for my room, that was enough to assist in that also. I had a room off campus. At that time it was very reasonable, so I didn't have a problem. I had saved some money from my years of working as a youngster going through high school.

Q: With all those jobs you had, there was certainly an opportunity.

Mr. Sublett: Oh, yes, yes. I had a pretty fair bank account at that time. My little savings bank was here until one of my kids played with it too strongly, I guess, and broke it. There was a date on tape on the bottom of

---

*The National Youth Administration (NYA) was established in 1935 as a New Deal employment measure. It had two principal objectives: providing part-time jobs for out-of-school young people and filling community needs. The program sought to instill good work habits and to provide skills and experience that would be useful for young people seeking full-time jobs.

Sublett #2 - 92

it--1929, the First National Bank of Highland Park. That's where I still bank.

Q: That's quite a record of longevity.

Mr. Sublett: That was.

Q: One thing that you mentioned when we talked the first time was your experience at Fort Riley, Kansas. If you could go into some more detail about that, please.

Mr. Sublett: This Citizens Military Training Camp was something I wanted to do, because my fellow students in high school were going away. They had money enough to go away every year to a summer camp up in Wisconsin, Minnesota, or wherever their families could send them, and I didn't have the money for that. This CTMC was offered to anyone who was qualified physically and mentally to get into it. The camp lasted for about three weeks, and it cost nothing for me to get into.

Q: This is sponsored by the government?

Mr. Sublett: Sponsored by the government for youth who could not afford anything different.

Sublett #2 - 93

Q: Who paid for the transportation?

Mr. Sublett: The government. And it was drilling, and we slept in huge tents. All the people running the camp were regular soldiers. Fort Riley was a cavalry outfit at that time, I believe, but we never saw a horse or rode one. The group that I was with was all marching and mostly for discipline and physical growth. That's what it was about. I guess all the type training we had was hiking, drilling, and drilling, of course, basically is training for discipline.

Q: Did your uncle's army experience have any factor in your going there?

Mr. Sublett: No, not particularly. I just wanted to go to maybe beef up a little bit and get some experience that would help me be a better athlete.

Q: And that enhanced your marksmanship as well.

Mr. Sublett: It definitely did, yes. Shooting on the rifle range was fun with a .30-.30 Springfield rifle. And I felt like, "Gee whiz, I'm a kid and these guys are men, and I'm right here with them." I was proud of my past experience as a kid, learning how to shoot as well as I

Sublett #2 - 94

could. Because I did very well.

Q: You probably have good hand-eye coordination.

Mr. Sublett: Yes, that had a lot to do with it, and we played games out there, of course. It was awfully hot. That was the only thing that I disliked about it. We wore woolen clothing, which I later found was the thing to do in extremely hot weather. I mean, 110° was more than I liked, but I tolerated it.

Q: Were these army uniforms?

Mr. Sublett: Army uniforms, yes--the army hat, the leggings, the whole bit.

Q: Smokey the Bear type hat?

Mr. Sublett: That's the type. Exactly.

Q: Well, you had professional instruction in your rifle shooting then.

Mr. Sublett: Oh, yes. Definitely so. We had the army rifles. Corporals usually were in charge.

Sublett #2 - 95

Q: Was your eyesight particularly good?

Mr. Sublett: It was.

Q: I can imagine that a motive for the Army in providing that training was to interest youngsters into going into the Army later, because there was no draft at that time.

Mr. Sublett: Well, at that time there could have been an instigation for making people interested in the Army. Let's see, I was 16. That was quite early on. And, after all, there was no conflicts in the world at that time that we would be involved in, or even thinking about. I don't know how big an Army they had during peacetime. I know I used to see the Army come by here from Fort Sheridan.* There was a cavalry outfit, also. They'd go down to Soldier Field for some sort of a show or a display.** I'd see all the mules and horses and caissons and all the equipment they had in those days. I also used to go past the naval training station at Great Lakes, and I saw what they had up there. So they were not recruiting, but, nevertheless, it could be something to try to make one interested in the service.

―――――――――――
*Fort Sheridan is an army post about eight miles north of Sublett's home in Glencoe, Illinois.
**Soldier Field is a large football stadium in downtown Chicago. Built in the 1920s, it is now the home field of the Chicago Bears of the National Football League.

Sublett #2 - 96

Q: Well, just like sea cadets today, for example. You expose somebody to something and maybe the interest develops.

Mr. Sublett: Yes, right. The only service-minded things in those days, I guess, were the ROTC for the Army and the Citizens Military Training Camp.

Q: Do you think that the experience at Fort Riley was any factor in steering you away from the Army when the war came?

Mr. Sublett: No, because I really enjoyed what I did at that summer camp. I loved it. But it had no bearing. I wanted to go to the Navy. Originally I wanted to go in the Air Corps. I wanted to be a flier. But there was nothing there for me.

Q: John Reagan had the same ambition.

Mr. Sublett: I was larger than I was supposed to be. And I worked hard to get down to 190 pounds, which was the limit. Then, after I did that, they only had one airfield for training blacks. That was at Tuskegee, Alabama. They had opened up the other facilities in the Navy for blacks.

Sublett #2 - 97

And I enlisted in the Navy.

Q: Back in your time at the University of Wisconsin, what was the racial climate there?

Mr. Sublett: Oh, much like it was in high school, very much.

There was one other black who went to Wisconsin that I knew of at that time from Illinois. There were some from other parts of the country, but very, very sparsely settled with blacks. I don't know what the attitude was, but there wasn't a big population of blacks.

Q: Nothing that inspired any militancy on your part?

Mr. Sublett: None whatsoever, no.

Q: Why did you move to the three different colleges?

Mr. Sublett: Well, first of all, I needed help after Wisconsin. I needed to bolster up my grades; that's why I went to Northwestern. And then I thought I was getting into education. That's why I went to George Williams College. They were known for their social work and medical work, and I thought surely I might be interested in that field, too.

Sublett #2 - 98

I knew some youngsters who were going there who were studying to be doctors; some were social workers; some got into the YMCA programs; some were in Hull House, Addams House, other public service places like that.* And I thought that might help, but my main reason for leaving Wisconsin was to get away from the athletics and study.

Q: You didn't have the opportunity to just study at Wisconsin without playing ball?

Mr. Sublett: Well, I could have, but that's what I went there for, and that's what they were so-called paying me for. I did well at football, except I wasn't satisfied with what I was doing in the classroom, so I had to change.

Q: Were the sports taking up too much time?

Mr. Sublett: Absolutely. As a matter of fact, I had to cut out track, because the football coach required you to go to spring football practice. It's much like today--one sport at a time.

---

*Hull House was one of the first social settlements in the United States. It was founded in Chicago in 1889 by Ellen Gates Starr and Jane Addams. Facilities included a day nursery, gymnasium, community kitchen, and a boarding club for working girls. It provided services and cultural opportunity for the immigrant population of the neighborhood and offered training for young social workers.

Q: The Big Ten was certainly one of the most prestigious conferences in the country back then. How well did you compete at that level?

Mr. Sublett: Average, just average. I wasn't outstanding.

Q: Do memories of any particular games stand out in your mind?

Mr. Sublett: Not particularly. I was in and out, substituting here and there. I do remember one little man who blocked me in the groin. He was about 165 pounds, and I weighed 220. He pulled out at guard and blocked me. He didn't knock me out but gave me a hell of a bang.

Q: Well, really, you didn't have a chance to find out how good you could be, because in the junior and senior years, presumably you would have had a better shot.

Mr. Sublett: Exactly true. There was a little bit of politics in that, too, in that area. Most of the kids who played were from the Wisconsin area. The alumni did not pull in too many people from the other states, and that hurt the team as a whole actually. And in later years the alumni changed that and pulled in more people from out of state. But their home state team boys were the favorites.

Sublett #2 - 100

Q: Who was the coach?

Mr. Sublett: Stuhldreher was the head coach.*

Q: One of the four horsemen of Notre Dame.

Mr. Sublett: Exactly. Right.

Q: Any memories of him?

Mr. Sublett: Oh, I just remember him up on the tower belting out his orders, that's all, and looking it over. Each group had their own coaches. Like the ends had theirs; the guards and running backs, theirs.

My first coach was Guy Sundt. He was good; good coach for a freshman. And then I had to give it up.

Q: Martin said he didn't feel that he got to play as much at Indiana as his ability warranted.** Did you have that feeling?

---
*Harry Stuhldreher was head football coach at the University of Wisconsin, 1936-48. In the early 1920s, he was quarterback for the Notre Dame Fighting Irish. He and his fellow backs Jim Crowley, Don Miller, and Elmer Layden became well known as the Four Horseman of Notre Dame after publication of a newspaper article by Grantland Rice.
**This is a reference to the oral history of Graham Martin, one of the members of the Golden Thirteen.

Sublett #2 - 101

Mr. Sublett: I felt the same way. As a youngster I used to watch Bernie Jefferson at Northwestern.* I thought he should have played more. But there were a few others that excelled and should have been recognized more than they were.

Q: Martin said that he got to play more away games than home games. Was that your experience?

Mr. Sublett: That's true, too. But I don't regret any of it at all. I just regret that I couldn't have gone on and played to my full potential in the junior and senior years, that's all. The pattern was as it was. I couldn't change it.

Q: Well, if you weren't getting your fair opportunity, that makes it easier to give it up.

Mr. Sublett: That's true, too.
   I knew one other black, and he gave it up the first year. He went on to journalism, and he's doing all right.

Q: Who was that?

---
*Jefferson was a back for Northwestern University in the late 1930s.

Sublett #2 - 102

Mr. Sublett: His name was Lester Brownley. He went into the Army, the last I heard of him.

Q: Do you think that this lack of a firm goal affected your college career in these several moves?

Mr. Sublett: It might have. It could have contributed to the fact that I didn't set myself up for a definite future. I was thinking along the terms of premed or something in that area but wasn't certain. I think everyone was taking basically a B.A. course, anyway, at that time. And that's the way it should be. I think when a youngster knows beforehand what he's going to do when he comes out of college, a B.A. is about all you need. It's for learning how to study, anyway. It's a continuation of the study methods learned in high school.

Q: Did your study habits improve as you went along?

Mr. Sublett: A bit, yes. I think it might have been even better if I would have had to pay my full freight all the way through, to appreciate what I was there for and why I'd spend my money for it.

Q: That's an interesting observation.

Mr. Sublett: You bet. I mean, some things that come easy, go easy. And it was easy going--up until that time it just continued to be a routine thing. So it might have helped if I had been a little bit more conscious of why. And had I paid for it, it might have helped a great deal.

Q: Do you think it likely that you would have finished college had the war not come along when it did?

Mr. Sublett: I would have. Yes. The only reason I didn't after the war was that when I was out in the Pacific, my mother-in-law wrote and told me to come home after I had gotten enough points and enough time to get out. They needed me at home. Well, it didn't work out anyway, because my wife and I split up after 15 years.* So it would have been better staying in. I wanted to. I liked the Navy that much. And then my father-in-law offered me a job down in the city. He was an alderman in Evanston, working in politics and I didn't want to get into it. So I would have much rather stayed in the Navy.

Q: Did your mother-in-law have that much clout?

Mr. Sublett: My mother-in-law thought I needed to come home and be with my wife. And we had a son at that time.

―――――――
*Mr. Sublett and his first wife were divorced in 1959.

Sublett #2 - 104

She felt that I should be there to help.

It wasn't the right thing for me to do, as I look back.

Q: It's ironic that some marriages break up from separation and some from togetherness.

Mr. Sublett: Right. Exactly right. She now lives in Lansing, Michigan. And my daughter lives up there near her. We had three children. As a matter of fact, I even tried it again with her, but that didn't work out either.

Q: Some couples are just destined not to get along.

Mr. Sublett: That's right. Exactly right. She went for the bright lights and hoopla. I like just plain living.

Q: It's interesting what a factor luck plays in one's life all along the course of it.

Mr. Sublett: Isn't it? Absolutely.

Q: Well, you told me before that a thing that steered you to the Navy was a love of the water, and you told me some things this morning that contributed to that, the fishing and the swimming and so forth.

Sublett #2 - 105

Mr. Sublett: That's very true. All of my children went through swimming class when they were old enough, because I did not want them to be afraid of water. I wanted them to know how to swim and protect themselves. They all love water, and they are terrific swimmers, always have been. I was swimming since I was a little kid. I was down at the beach every day. So I did love it, and I still love the water. I got rid of my canoe only because I thought nobody would use it again. Otherwise I'd have it here to take it out for a ride once in a while. I used to take it camping. The kids lost interest in that sort of thing. I don't know if they even go swimming anymore.

Q: We've talked about some bad luck. Some good luck was that the general service ratings opened up in the Navy at a time when you were likely to be drafted otherwise.

Mr. Sublett: That is exactly true. I did not want any part of the Army, and that's why I selected the Navy. That was my preference. And then after taking my aptitude test, I was qualified to become a machinist's mate. And that would take me down into the engine room of a ship. I loved engines and mechanical things like that. I love them, because I had been experienced with automobiles a lot. And I just loved the water.

Sublett #2 - 106

Q: I'd be interested in more about your experiences at boot camp. You talked about the hammocks before. What was the routine at boot camp?

Mr. Sublett: The routine at boot camp was drilling, of course, and cleanliness, seamanship--tying knots, nautical nomenclature, knowing what a ship looks like, and trying to identify the various ships and planes of the Navy. And then learning how to handle small arms. I don't recall now whether we had a rifle to shoot or not. But we drilled without rifles. I called the cadence at that time. We had chief petty officers who were the commanding officers of our boot camp companies.

Q: These were white guys.

Mr. Sublett: White chiefs, yes. I was assistant to the chief in charge of our company, to help these other recruits to be clean and to learn the other basics of boot camp.

Q: Because you were more experienced?

Mr. Sublett: Perhaps they saw that in my qualities, yes.

Sublett #2 - 107

Q: How much help did these fellows need?

Mr. Sublett: Some needed a lot, because they came from places where they'd never seen big bodies of water. They knew how to tie knots, but not a type of knot the Navy required. And cleanliness was far from their reach in some areas. They came from farms; they came from hills, mountain country. They were all black, by the way. We did not have a mixed group in our boot camp. And some could not read well. They needed remedial help, which was later introduced at Great Lakes, but, in fact, didn't have a lot to do in that expression at boot camp.

Q: It sounds like you were a sort of big brother to some of these guys.

Mr. Sublett: That's one good way of putting it, yes. That's right.

Q: And I can imagine, knowing you, that it was sympathetically done rather than harshly.

Mr. Sublett: It was not a forceful thing. It was to help if I could. And that situation was recognized because later the Navy provided a remedial study group.

Sublett #2 - 108

Q: Mr. Williams told me yesterday that he had a big hand in getting that going, and Nelson was involved in that also.*

Mr. Sublett: Definitely Nelson, because he had been a teacher down in Tennessee. And Mummy did have something in that area to do with it, I believe. And it was very helpful.

Q: Did you enjoy the boot camp experience?

Mr. Sublett: I did. I enjoyed every minute I spent in the Navy, every minute of it. Absolutely. I felt sorry for some of the young guys who did not do as they were supposed to do and caused a lousy inspection or something like that. As a punishment they had to stand out in the sun or walk on the parade grounds.

Everything that happened to me in the Navy was a plus, so I have a real positive attitude about it.

Q: How early in the scheme of things did you become the assistant to the chief?

Mr. Sublett: Maybe a couple weeks, something like that.

---
*Lewis R. Williams was one of the enlisted men who went through the officer training program but was not commissioned. Dennis D. Nelson II was a member of the Golden Thirteen.

It was after enough time for him to recognize the values or the talents of all of us.

Q: Being the easygoing guy you are, was it tough to impose the necessary discipline?

Mr. Sublett: No, not at all. I didn't get any disrespect from anybody. They totally realized they needed it, and so they fell right in with it. There were a couple of occasions that I kind of put some men in the shower to show them what cleanliness is, but that wasn't too bad either.

Q: That's a navy tradition.

Mr. Sublett: That's right. That wasn't something that I thought up. It had to be done, and that was the old way of doing it.

Q: How would you describe the attitude and enthusiasm of the men in the boot camp?

Mr. Sublett: Oh, there was a lot of grumbling and griping. I mean, there were so many who did not like discipline. Most of them were drafted, and they didn't want to be there in the first place. So they had a negative attitude about

Sublett #2 - 110

the entire setup. And some did not like to be told what to do, when to do it, how to do it. That created some problems, so they had to be reprimanded, and I don't remember how it was done at that time. I mean, it was too early for brig. There was nothing that serious at that time, so some extra duty was probably the punishment.

Q: That has a deterrent effect after it's imposed once or twice.

Mr. Sublett: Right. It does.

Q: Did the chief treat you with respect and dignity?

Mr. Sublett: As I recall, he did, yes. I don't remember anything that would cause me to remember that he didn't.

Q: You went from boot camp to Hampton. What was the atmosphere like there? Could you see an improvement in quality and attitude?

Mr. Sublett: Well, yes, there was definitely a difference, because the men that went to Hampton had been selected out of boot camp to further advance in different areas, like machinist's mate and electrician's mate, metalsmith, and that sort of thing. We had all been tested and qualified

Sublett #2 - 111

to go to Hampton.

Q: So these were all people who had all been successful.

Mr. Sublett: That's right. We were the first company to go to Hampton, the company that I went in, and John Reagan was with me. We were the only two out of the officer training group that were together at that time. The other fellows stayed at Great Lakes.

Q: Was Cooper at Hampton then?

Mr. Sublett: Cooper was an instructor at that time. I think that's when I first met George--one of the nicest guys in the world. He really was, and still is.

And the attitude was definitely better there, because we had a different makeup of people. Some had been teachers; some worked for newspapers or publishers; some had been in the medical field or were getting into it. These were students who were better qualified than the others that did not pass. I don't know where they ever shipped out the other men.

Q: Would you have any guess as to the attrition rate, how many didn't make it through the service school?

Sublett #2 - 112

Mr. Sublett: No, I have no idea how many didn't.

Q: Was your work graded on a regular basis, tests and so forth?

Mr. Sublett: I don't recall that. I don't know how that was handled.

Q: Did you have a sense at the time that you had moved into some sort of an elite group at Hampton?

Mr. Sublett: No, I just figured it was like going to another grade. I didn't feel that it was elite at all. As a matter of fact, I didn't think it when I went to the officers' training school. I had no idea about that either.

Q: That's curious.

Mr. Sublett: This thing didn't soak in to me until after we were reunionized.

Q: So you were just taking one thing at a time.

Mr. Sublett: That's it. I felt I was going to Hampton to study something that I wanted to do. And it was a new

Sublett #2 - 113

vista.

Q: How capable were the instructors there?

Mr. Sublett: Mr. Antoine was a real good instructor. I think I remember him as a machinist's mate instructor. He was very knowledgeable and had been there for quite some time and was well experienced in teaching.

Q: Was he a civilian?

Mr. Sublett: He was a civilian, yes.

Q: That's how George Cooper started off there initially, and then he later became a chief petty officer.

Mr. Sublett: That is right, yes. He did go to school there.

Q: What specifics do you remember from the training at Hampton?

Mr. Sublett: Commander Downes was in charge of the whole thing. And he was quite proud of what he was doing there. He was a real leader. Some of the guys used to say "the great white father" about Commander Armstrong up at Great

Sublett #2 - 114

Lakes. I guess Downes was the same type of a figure in Hampton, Virginia, except that he was a different, a little bit softer character than Armstrong. But he wanted to do well; he wanted all of us to do well.

After our first company, some more companies came along, enough to create a battalion. I was the battalion commander for our inspections and parades. For anything formal I was in charge and second to Commander Downes.

Q: How much contact did you have with him?

Mr. Sublett: I had real good contact with Commander Downes. I learned a lot from him. He personally called my mother, and he told her how I was doing there. I was doing well and that sort of thing. And he wrote to her, also.

He talked with each one of us, asked us our names--this is in our introduction with him--and where we were from and what schooling we had gone through. And the next time I talked with Commander Downes, he knew exactly my name, where I was from, and what schools I had attended--all that I told him before--without hesitation. All of us were asked that information.

Q: George Cooper was very impressed by that same quality in him.

Sublett #2 - 115

Mr. Sublett: Really remarkable man.

Q: Besides being a good memory trick, it shows a concern for you as an individual.

Mr. Sublett: He was definitely concerned, right. I don't know how he could remember all those people. Maybe he did not do all of them. Those who he picked out to remember or know as much as he could about them, but he knew what he had asked.

Q: Well, certainly he didn't have to make the call to your mother.

Mr. Sublett: No, he didn't have to. It was unbelievable how he did that.

But he did want us to be successful. He pounded that time after time--to be good <u>men</u>. We were <u>men</u> of Hampton, and he wanted to make us realize that we were <u>men</u>, to be <u>good men</u> all the way through, no matter what we did. He was a real father actually.

Q: He instilled pride and dignity.

Mr. Sublett: He did. He wanted that outstandingly.

Sublett #2 - 116

Q: Cooper draws a real distinction between Downes and Armstrong in their styles of leadership.

Mr. Sublett: I would not compare, because I don't know much about Armstrong. I have no way of knowing too much about him. What I've heard, to me it's negative compared to Commander Downes. But I had no dealings with Commander Armstrong. He was a Great Lakes man, and Nelson and Arbor and the Barneses--all those fellows had a lot to do with him.

Q: And certainly Goodwin.

Mr. Sublett: Goodwin, yes. And White. But Reagan and myself were down at Hampton with Commander Downes, and he was our mentor.

Q: Did you have any contact with Dalton Baugh during that period?

Mr. Sublett: No, I didn't. The first time I met Dalton was at officers' training school, and that's the last contact I had until the reunion.

Q: Do you remember any specifics about working with equipment at Hampton? Did they have training aids to use?

Sublett #2 - 117

Mr. Sublett: It was mostly improvised, although we went over to Norfolk occasionally to see what a real navy base looked like, what navy ships looked like, and that sort of thing.

We had small boats--the captain's gig and maybe a whaleboat or two, or something like that, in the Hampton Roads that were available to us. That's how we got further seamanship. I used to teach small boat handling a little bit when we were there. And to get acquainted with the real Navy we went over to Norfolk; Commander Downes saw to that. The school also had all sorts of physical training equipment--obstacle courses and that sort of thing.

Q: Did you have good books to study from?

Mr. Sublett: Very good books, topnotch books. And he had a good staff of instructors there. I'm trying to think of who they were, but I can't at the moment.

Q: Did you get to go aboard any of the ships over at Norfolk?

Mr. Sublett: No, because we were black, you know. And they had steward's mates and cooks and all that sort of thing, but they didn't have any real integration. Downes knew where to go and where we couldn't.

Q: He knew what the limits were.

Mr. Sublett: Absolutely. Sure.

Q: Certainly Norfolk has a much different racial climate than where you had grown up. What were your experiences ashore?

Mr. Sublett: Didn't go ashore. Newport News was the farthest I ever went off campus and that was to the house of some acquaintance. I think Cooper even lived on campus at that time and his family. But on campus was as far as I went. I didn't want to stray even to a movie house in town. They had movies on campus, so I could look at them, but I didn't have any desire to go roaming around anywhere there. I mean, Fort Eustis was not too far away. That was an army base. And there were people there who used to come over, because they knew some of the girls and boys on campus at Hampton.

Q: Did you have any interaction with the civilian students at Hampton?

Mr. Sublett: Just all friendly attitudes and that sort.

Sublett #2 - 119

Nothing unpleasant. It was all favorable and they were glad to see us there and to know what we were there for.

Q: And from there up to Boston.

Mr. Sublett: From there I went to Boston. That was my first experience aboard a floating craft, if you would call it that.*

Q: How big would you say it was?

Mr. Sublett: Oh, what would it be? About 20-footer, 25 maybe.

They had a chief who had been in the Bay area there on a fishing boat. It might have been his; I don't know. We had a white cook and one other seaman there. I was a machinist's mate; one other machinist's mate came aboard later. I was the first one to go.

This boat was equipped with sonar gear. Even though I was rated as a machinist's mate, the only thing I did aboard that ship was listen for submarines and that sort of thing. We did have a kind of little diesel engine, which was problem-free. They had a machinist's mate take care of that. He was white also.

―――――――――
*Mr. Sublett's records indicate that the craft was a converted fishing boat named the Queen of Peace (A-45).

Sublett #2 - 120

Q: Was it a harmonious living arrangement?

Mr. Sublett: It was okay. It was so small it had to be harmonious. I mean, you go out and take your shift and listen, and monitor your findings, which were nil. Nobody slipped into the Bay, and so we had no activity.

Q: The Germans weren't very adventuresome at that point.

Mr. Sublett: At that point they were not. Absolutely.

Q: Wasn't that rather boring to go out day after day?

Mr. Sublett: It was. I mean, that's the way it was day after day, because we tied up every night and slept in the barracks on the pier.

Q: Well, you probably shot the breeze with these guys to pass the day.

Mr. Sublett: Oh, you'd shoot the breeze--sure, you do.

Q: What was life like in the barracks?

Mr. Sublett: It was okay. They had recreational equipment

Sublett #2 - 121

in there. And each morning you'd get up and do your calisthenics and go to chow and make your bunks. There wasn't any time to clean. They had a cleaning crew for that.

Q: That was really your first integrated experience in the Navy, wasn't it?

Mr. Sublett: It was, right there on the base, and on that boat, too.

Q: Did it go well?

Mr. Sublett: It was okay. It went well. There were no problems there. There were guys from Philadelphia, and there were guys from Virginia--black guys, I mean. And they were from various places. And it all went well.

I remember one young man who used to play the saxophone, and he had it with him. And there were pool shooters, and there were crap shooters and, you know, a mixture of everything. And there were intellects who wanted to read. It was all right. It was okay.

After I left that boat, I went back to the base to the machine shop. And there I worked out on the machines--the lathes and so forth--making propeller shafts and repairing or making propellers and other auxiliary engine components.

Sublett #2 - 122

Q: Had blueprint reading been part of your training at service school?

Mr. Sublett: A little. Enough to get by and to repair or make small engine parts. Yes.

Q: Did you go on liberty in Boston?

Mr. Sublett: Yes, I did. Went on liberty--went to Boston Common, the Revere Beach, Copley Square, theaters, restaurants, shops, and met other naval personnel from other areas, other ships. And that was quite interesting. They did not know too much about regular Navy people other than the steward's mates and cooks and that sort of thing. So we were all new to them, also.

Q: I've talked to a number of the servicemen from World War II, Navy men, who said that the public was very enthusiastic, would greet them warmly, buy them drinks and so forth. Did you find that?

Mr. Sublett: Well, not being a drinker at that time, I didn't have that kind of a relationship, but I did find them warm and friendly. Yes, we had nice associations up to the limit of socializing without drinking.

Sublett #2 - 123

Q: Did you develop some friends in that group?

Mr. Sublett: Acquaintances, I'll say. Yes. Some that now I have corresponded with. Well, I received correspondence from one particular young lady. She remembered my name and saw pictures after our commissioning. She wrote me a complimentary letter and said she was married to an army person. And that's the only thing I can recall. But I did make some friends in Boston area.

Q: I guess the point to be made is that you felt that the atmosphere in Boston was more hospitable than in Hampton so that you could get out.

Mr. Sublett: Well, I felt that way. Yes. And, of course, I visited Harvard University and saw the other cultural places, too, that were of interest. I liked Boston a lot. I was in and out of Boston for about a year, in the machine shop area mostly. That's how I got the liberty to go up into Boston proper.

Q: What are your recollections of the process of finding out about the trip to Great Lakes and your reaction to that?

Sublett #2 - 124

Mr. Sublett: My reaction to receiving orders to "Prepare your gear in seagoing fashion. You're going to ship out tomorrow morning," was nothing specifically surprising. I knew not why I was going to Great Lakes, so it was just another move to another duty. I had no idea of why I was going there or what I would be doing there.

Q: You had gotten into this tradition of following orders, so you did.

Mr. Sublett: Exactly right. Because I was told what to do and when, and that was it.

Q: What are your recollections of first getting into the barracks in the situation there at Great Lakes?

Mr. Sublett: Oh, I still didn't know anything after I got there. I had no idea what it was about.

Q: How long did it take?

Mr. Sublett: I was glad to meet all these new men. They were all new to me except Reagan, whom I hadn't seen since Hampton. It was nice, but I still didn't know what we were going to do or why we were there, or even if we were going to be in the same group doing anything together. It was

Sublett #2 - 125

several days before I really found out that we were there for officers' training class.

Q: Did the instructors give you any idea of why you were there?

Mr. Sublett: Well, I'm sure that fairly soon the instructors had told us why, or someone had told us why we were there and what was expected of us. And then that's when we fell right into the program.

Q: When did this business come about that you would all cooperate and pool your individual resources for the common good?

Mr. Sublett: That came about during our study sessions, knowing that we had these classes of navigation, navy regulations, and navy history, and all those subjects pertaining to Navy. We just pooled ourselves as one to help each other, and especially those who were weak in one subject others could help. And that's where we all had a very general knowledge of the entire program then. Some were better equipped with some subjects than others were. And we were willing and able to help each other that way to pull through. As long as we realized that we had to be together, we worked together.

Sublett #2 - 126

Q: Is that something that came about early in the course?

Mr. Sublett: I would say yes. Maybe it was after one test. That would probably be the most likely reason it would occur that way.

Q: How frequent were the tests?

Mr. Sublett: We were tested often, and in order to keep up to date with our progress, I'm sure it was regular.

Q: You probably compared grades, which is how you found out this need for some kind of a program.

Mr. Sublett: I don't recall if we ever knew our grades. I don't really know that.

Q: Well, then was it a case where somebody just thought that he did poorly on a test?

Mr. Sublett: Perhaps that, or the instructor might have indicated in some manner that somebody needed help, or we might have gotten grades. I don't remember that really. I have no record of it now. Or the grades might have been something that we initially saw and the instructors kept.

Sublett #2 - 127

Q: Do you recall whose idea it was to have this sharing of information?

Mr. Sublett: There was no one individual. I'm sure it just came about naturally. Maybe if I had a question, I would ask someone. And then if he didn't know, he would ask someone, and eventually we would find out who was best qualified to answer that question. And then we would know whom to go to for that type of question again. And then we just worked it that way--a matter of need.

Q: I gather it became more formalized as you went on.

Mr. Sublett: Well, yes, because after a length of time we knew who was more knowledgeable about one subject than some of the others.

Q: I got the impression from Mr. Arbor that the routine in the evening was that you would go through the subjects one by one, and the expert on that subject would deal with it.

Mr. Sublett: Well, if the occasion arose, I imagine it was that way. But we did study every day, every night, and we all studied the same subjects. But then I think the questions came up as needed. A particular one would take a course in navy regs and expound to all the others what it was all about, and I think there was more or less a question thing in what one didn't understand better.

Q: Did the instructors seem to know that this sharing of information was going on?

Mr. Sublett: Yes, I think they knew about it.

Q: And made no effort to stop it.

Mr. Sublett: There was no effort to stop it. I'm sure some of them were happy to see that we were enthusiastic about the program and wanted to be cooperative in that respect to help each other to attain that knowledge that we were supposed to.

Q: Did you have the feeling that the instructors were genuinely trying to help you?

Mr. Sublett: I had no reason not to think that. I thought they were all very helpful and gave us all the attention that they should have. If I remember correctly, I think we had a good bunch of instructors, a good team of helpful officers. I don't know what their qualifications were, but I think they made a genuinely good, honest attempt to teach

Sublett #2 - 129

us what we needed to know.

Q: Did you feel any sense of condescension from them?

Mr. Sublett: No. None at all.

Q: Did you get any sense that they felt that you weren't capable of handling the material?

Mr. Sublett: I didn't get that feeling at all. I think they respected us for what we knew and what we tried to do.

Q: At what point did you come to an awareness that you had been investigated by the FBI?

Mr. Sublett: I didn't know that until the program was over. I had no idea.

Q: And what was your reaction?

Mr. Sublett: I wasn't told directly. I don't know how that came about either.

My reaction was no problem. I hadn't any qualms about having been checked on my past life at all. Because I knew what I had been through, and there were no black spots in my life at all.

Sublett #2 - 130

Q: Mr. Cooper said he was bothered by it, because he felt that white officer candidates did not get similar investigations.

Mr. Sublett: Well, I didn't have any thoughts about that. I didn't begin to think of what the others had gone through.

After we had gotten into the program, I realized then that we were a different group from the whites, that the whites had been privileged to go through V-12 and V-7 programs and we were not, so we were different. And I knew it.

Q: Did you feel a sense of strangeness that you were not only separated from the white officer candidates but from the black sailors as well?

Mr. Sublett: No, I didn't feel any different about that.

Those were the people who we were going to lead, so to speak. If we were to become officers, I didn't expect them to put us among a group of white enlisted personnel. We all treated the black enlisted people with the due respect that they deserved.

Q: Did you have the feeling that this separate billeting

Sublett #2 - 131

in barracks for your group was to keep the information away from others of what was going on?

Mr. Sublett: No, I didn't feel that way. I figured they set that up for us specially because they didn't want us at Northwestern or the other colleges that were presenting the V-12 program. And they set it up specially, because they didn't have anywhere else to put it for us.

We were a separate group to begin with, and that's the way we were really treated, separately. I don't know whether they intended that we would make it or not. It was truly an experiment to see if we could take it and make it.

Q: Did you feel that they were trying to help you make it?

Mr. Sublett: I think they tried to help us make it, and they made it tough for us to make it. I feel good about the fact that we made it, because, being black, you have to excel in everything you do to be recognized. And you've got two strikes to start with, and if you take a third one, you're gone. So they make it tough. You have to be good.

Q: Tough in what ways?

Mr. Sublett: I mean at whatever you do. You have to be smart, intelligent in what field you're going to be in, and

Sublett #2 - 132

if it's athletics, you have to be twice as good as the other man in order to be recognized for your abilities. So that was it. And they made it tough so they'd be sure we qualified if we could go through the rough spells.

Q: Do you have any idea that it was tougher than the white curriculum or comparable?

Mr. Sublett: I would say it was comparable. I mean, it might have seemed tougher only because being the first blacks has to be an obstacle to begin with. And nobody knew where we were going. They offered this opportunity, but how many really expected us to go complete it? How many truly wanted us to is not known. So, on the whole, though, I believe everyone honestly tried to make it so that we could complete it successfully.

Q: So it was a legitimate opportunity?

Mr. Sublett: I believe it was legitimate. I believe that.

Q: One thing that would lead you to believe that is that good men were picked for it.

Mr. Sublett: Well, I think that also, and many, many times I've thought that, gee, 16 individuals taken out of

Sublett #2 - 133

120,000, as I understand. It seems to me there could have been another 16, or another 16 that could have gone through the program as successfully as we did. And, therefore, I am particularly grateful to have been a member of that first 16, because, as I said, I think there were a lot more guys just as capable as we were.

Q: Well, looking just at the numbers, Mr. Cooper said he got the feeling he was representing several thousand black enlisted men.

Mr. Sublett: That's what it amounted to, yes.

Q: Did you have a feeling of that sort of responsibility at the time you were going through the training?

Mr. Sublett: No, I did not. I felt that after I had completed the course. After I had successfully passed and gotten my commission, then I realized that, "Hey, I'm here," and we recognized it and carried ourselves accordingly.

Q: Did you have a feeling at the time that it was an experiment?

Mr. Sublett: I felt that it was, yes.

Sublett #2 - 134

Q: Did that put any pressure on the situation?

Mr. Sublett: None, not at all, no.

If you're going to experiment with something, you have to start out with something that you believe is true and can make it. So we had the basics and went from there.

Q: But did you contemplate the consequences of failure?

Mr. Sublett: No, I did not.

I didn't have that feeling about anybody in the group, as a matter of fact. I thought we were all capable. After knowing those men for a few weeks or so, I had no doubts in my mind about making the complete course successfully.

Q: There must have been moments, though, of uncertainty or pressure. Inevitably, people are going to get on each others' nerves. Did you have times like that?

Mr. Sublett: There were times like that, yes. During the course of study, or play, or whatever, there were instances of little anxieties, maybe. But then someone would come up with a quip or a turn of thought and change the entire feeling around, and that's one of the good things about the group.

Sublett #2 - 135

Q: I guess Arbor was especially good at that.

Mr. Sublett: Arbor was good at that, because Nelson would get testy occasionally, and then Arbor would come up with something real silly or goofy, and it would change the whole attitude. Somebody would laugh out--Phil Barnes was a real laugher--and that would create a different attitude. So you forget and start over, without thinking about it.

Q: Were there leaders within the group?

Mr. Sublett: Not particularly. I mean, leaders to the extent of knowing the personnel at Great Lakes, like Nelson and Goodwin who had been stationed there for some time, who had connections in the sense of whom to talk with or go to see about anything that might come up. But, no, there was no particular leader for our group, per se, for our program that we were going through.

Q: I wonder if you and John Reagan felt deferential at all since you were the youngest in the group.

Mr. Sublett: I don't think so. No, none at all. There was no feeling of a difference there at all.

Sublett #2 - 136

Q: So 16 equal men.

Mr. Sublett: Sixteen men, exactly.

Q: Was Lear treated any differently because he wasn't a college man?

Mr. Sublett: No, he was not. Lear was as regular as the rest of us. He mixed well in the group, and there was no difference in treatment toward him than there was with anyone else.

Q: Did he need more help than the others because of that?

Mr. Sublett: He did in some instances, yes. And another man there, Alves, did not have some of the education that we had, and he needed help. Eventually he didn't make it, anyway. He also had merchant marine experience, so he was helpful in his way.

Q: Others have mentioned you as being very helpful on mechanical-type things because of your background.

Mr. Sublett: That's, perhaps, true because I had worked in automobile shops and was interested in motors and that sort of thing. And I had been on duty out at the navy base in

Sublett #2 - 137

Boston with the small engines, auxiliary engines and so forth. And I went to the Bosch fuel injection school up in Springfield, Massachusetts; that furthered my interest and education in engines. So perhaps I could offer help in that field.

Q: What about gunnery? Did you have some knowledge in that?

Mr. Sublett: I had a lot of knowledge about gunnery and maybe I was helpful in that direction, too. We did shoot on the range there. We shot 20 millimeters, and they were beautiful. I liked the 40 millimeters also. But I had had a lot of previous experience with guns.

Q: None of you would have had any experience with the bigger guns, so you were probably all working from scratch there.

Mr. Sublett: We were all working from start on the bigger guns. The 20 millimeter and the 40 millimeter were just fabulous to shoot--Chicago piano, they called it, pompoms or whatever. They were beautiful antiaircraft guns. And that was fun, great fun.

Q: There's so much solidarity in the group now that it's

Sublett #2 - 138

almost literally like brothers. Was it like that then?

Mr. Sublett: It's probably stronger now. Absolutely. We had a good unit then, but we were beginners at that time. We were learning each other. And we grew quickly to one, to a nucleus of one group, or one unit, rather, to work together, and it worked out beautifully.

Q: Did you have much contact with Commander Armstrong?

Mr. Sublett: I had very little with Commander Armstrong. No more than acknowledgement of "Good morning, sir," or something like that.

Q: How frequently would that be?

Mr. Sublett: That was very rare. He was over on the main side of the complex, and we were over on the other side--Camp Robert Smalls. I think he did have an office over on our side, but I had no reason to go there for anything.

Q: The way it was set up, I gather everything came to you.

Mr. Sublett: It did. Absolutely.

Q: The instructors came your building.

Sublett #2 - 139

Mr. Sublett: They did. We were confined to one particular barracks for all our studies--for all our needs except for outside athletics, like the obstacle course and recreational . . .

Q: Did your group have the whole barracks to itself?

Mr. Sublett: Yes, we did--if I recall correctly.

Q: There must have been a lot of unused space then.

Mr. Sublett: There was, I'm sure. I don't remember the entire structure of it completely. But we did have one complete barracks to ourselves.

Q: And then you went somewhere else to eat, I guess.

Mr. Sublett: Yes, we went to a mess hall to eat. And we ate by ourselves. We were not with another group of people. Like I said, everything we did was just our little group as one.

Q: Did you march?

Mr. Sublett: No, I think our drilling days were completed

before that.

Q: You probably marched to chow.

Mr. Sublett: Maybe we marched to chow and back, but so far as parade drilling, no, we didn't have that.

Q: I would think that the physical activity would be a really welcome thing in that kind of environment.

Mr. Sublett: Definitely to get out and relax and loosen up a bit, toss a ball, or whatever, swimming. We had to go through the swimming tests, too, and we went through the obstacle courses again, as we did when we went through boots. It was relaxing indeed to get out and loosen up on our recreational period.

Q: Were you already engaged at that point?

Mr. Sublett: Yes.

Q: How much communication could you have with your future wife?

Mr. Sublett: We communicated by telephone, and it was convenient for her parents to drive her up to talk through

Sublett #2 - 141

the fence outside the gate.

Q: What would be the routine for a typical day during your course of study?

Mr. Sublett: Oh, my, this is really pulling hard now, trying to think of some of the activities or what, or how the routine went. I know I did and a few others did morning exercise individually. Some got up and studied and read a little bit until chow. And then back to the books after morning chow and study until break time at noon chow, back to the books from 1300 until afternoon break.

Q: Were the classes every day?

Mr. Sublett: We had classes every day.

Q: Was the routine different on weekends?

Mr. Sublett: I'm sure we got a break on weekends. Come to think of it, I might have gotten a chance to come home once or twice during the weekends, because I lived close by, and so it was possible that I did come home then.

Q: Was the environment oppressive?

Sublett #2 - 142

Mr. Sublett: Oppressive? No. As I've told many people, I said, "If I could do it all over again, I would." My entire career in the Navy was one that I would do again. I enjoyed my entire tour of duty in the Navy from start to finish.

Q: The thing you would change probably is to have more of it.

Mr. Sublett: That's exactly right. I would definitely have preferred more of it. I'm sorry that I terminated it when I did.

Q: What uniforms did you wear during that training?

Mr. Sublett: We wore our Navy enlisted men's uniform. They were called undress blues and were just plain without white piping on the jumpers. The pants were bell bottoms.

Q: Did you wear the standard white hat?

Mr. Sublett: We did.

Q: Do you have any specific recollections of instructors?

Mr. Sublett: No.

Sublett #2 - 143

Q: Did you have any clues on Pinkney and Alves and why they didn't get commissioned?

Mr. Sublett: No. I liked Alves because he had had previous experience in the merchant marines. I talked a lot with Alves about some of his experiences and so forth. But I don't know why he didn't make it. And Pinkney, I don't have any idea about him either. As far as I can remember, they were as regular as the rest of the fellows were in the class. And their work was as good, and they had as much to contribute in their fields or backgrounds as the others had, so I just don't know.

Q: It would be interesting to know if there are some records somewhere that would explain that.

Mr. Sublett: There probably are, but there were none for us, because they didn't even give us a graduation certificate. They had no kind of a ceremony of completing the class at all. I think we were called in individually and told we were ensigns: "You're an officer of the Navy now," or whatever, and then we got the official seal, I guess, indicating that we successfully completed the course.

Sublett #2 - 144

Q: Was this Armstrong that talked to you individually?

Mr. Sublett: I don't remember that. I have no idea. He might have, and he might have designated it to his XO.* I don't know.

Q: Do you remember taking an oath as an ensign, being sworn in?

Mr. Sublett: No, the only oath I ever took was when I first enlisted in the Navy. That was it. I don't recall taking any other than that.

Q: What do you remember of the process getting your ensign's uniforms?

Mr. Sublett: Oh, I guess we were told where to go and buy them, and that was it. I think they told us how much allowance we'd have for a uniform. My first trip was down at a store in Chicago. I bought blue uniforms for the Navy at ship's service. Finchley was the name of the store. I went down there and they had all the equipment that I needed for my uniform. I bought a uniform there, a topcoat and a scarf, and I still have the scarf. I wore the topcoat until it was worn. And I still have the uniform,

---

*XO--executive officer.

Sublett #2 - 145

also.

Q: What was your emotional reaction when you found out that you had made it?

Mr. Sublett: Oh, I was proud that I had passed the course, and that I had made it to become an officer. It was another advance for me in the Navy. I didn't fully realize the impact that it really initiated by becoming an officer. And it didn't for a long time, because so many people didn't know that I was an officer in the Navy. Especially the blacks, they did not know an ensign from a ship's cook, or a ship's steward. So it was quite some time, I guess, before I really felt the proudness that I should have.

Q: The Navy didn't really give you that opportunity.

Mr. Sublett: Well, no, they didn't. A diploma would have helped, or anything that would encourage you to realize what you had done, and what you can do further. I felt that they didn't know what to do with us after they had commissioned us.

Q: Well, this is a view that Mr. Williams expressed yesterday, that the Navy had been forced by a lot of pressure to do this.

Mr. Sublett: I believe that.

Q: And that it was merely window dressing.

Mr. Sublett: That's exactly the way I looked at it. There have been so many rumors as to how it came about since the installation of blacks into the regular Navy above deck and below decks opportunities, that it was just something to further the movement of the blacks, and who encouraged it, I don't know. I've heard it was Mrs. Roosevelt, and then in line of command, President Roosevelt down to the Secretary of the Navy. And I don't know if it was NAACP or the Urban League or who else encouraged that.* But all of those combined, I'm sure, had some effect on the movement then carried out by the President's command.

Q: Did you want to go aboard ship?

Mr. Sublett: I wanted to badly. You bet. I didn't want to get a commission in the Navy and be a qualified deck officer, a line officer, and then do something else that was not closely related. I wanted to be involved in the combat area after learning responsibilities aboard a fighting ship. That's what I wanted to be into, but I

---
*NAACP--National Association for the Advancement of Colored People.

Sublett #2 - 147

never got that opportunity.

Q: No, the Navy said, "The opportunity stops here."

Mr. Sublett: That is it. They did not know where to put us and what to do with us, so my first assignment after being commissioned was down at Hampton Institute to train other men in what I had gone through.

Q: Was it truly a more responsible assignment than you'd had as an enlisted man?

Mr. Sublett: No, it was not more, because I taught the same things that I taught before I was commissioned. It was the uniform that probably made a difference to the young men who were being taught that it was a matter of respect. That's all it amounted to.

Q: Could you detect an increased amount of pride on their part?

Mr. Sublett: Yes, there was definitely, because the men at Hampton understood better than the outside world. I mean, the man on the street, the sailor on the street, cooks, bakers or whatever, people who were the underprivileged, so to speak, did not know.

Q: One thing that you did for those sailors, though, you gave them something to shoot for that you hadn't had.

Mr. Sublett: I was a role model, active role model, for them, true enough. And in that respect, they gained a lot, knowing what was achievable if they were in a capacity to take advantage of all the opportunities that they had at that time. And that's what we're trying to instill in these youngsters today. They need to know more today, because they have greater opportunities. It's there for them. All they need to do is reach out and get it. There are so many kids today who are qualified to go through any of the NROTCs, get a commission, learn a career if they don't do the officer program. And come out and be good citizens in a good country for a good cause.

Q: And the Naval Academy was unheard of then for blacks.

Mr. Sublett: No, you didn't even mention that. I mean, the Naval Academy played Army in football. That was the extent of Naval Academy knowledge then for us. That was a game to look forward to, but who ever heard of a black man in the Naval Academy? There may have been one or two in West Point.

Sublett #2 - 149

Q: Yes, there were.

Mr. Sublett: But certainly not in the Navy.

But, anyway, these young men were appreciative of why we were there, and they respected us.

Q: Did you encounter white sailors also during that period?

Mr. Sublett: Oh, I did, but still I didn't have any cause to go out ashore on liberty too much, because of all the facilities we had there. We had boats to fool around with--sailboats and motorboats to play around in. There was time to teach. We had programs for entertainment right on campus. At all times there was something to do. So I didn't have any real cause to go ashore. I would sometimes go to visit Cooper's house.

Q: How much contact did you have with him and Reagan while you were there as officers?

Mr. Sublett: As officers Reagan and I were together a lot, and Cooper, also. Cooper had a home on campus; he and his wife were very gracious to us at all times. I'll never forget--that's where I had my first drink of Southern

Comfort.

But so far as white sailors, a sailor was a sailor. When I went ashore and saw one, if he saluted, okay. If he didn't, okay. I wasn't expecting them to do any more than anyone else. I mean, some of the blacks didn't salute because they didn't know any different either. So that sort of thing never bothered me, whether somebody saluted me or not. It wasn't that person-to-person thing, anyway. I mean, I was wearing a United States Navy uniform. That was due the respect, not particularly because I was wearing it. It all depends on how much you feel for your cause, you know, being an American.

Q: Another way to look at it, it's not just the uniform but that you have earned the right to wear that uniform.

Mr. Sublett: Well, that I had proven by wearing it, and if they chose to respect that, fine. And if they didn't, they didn't. Some didn't know any better and some were begrudgingly aware of it and cared, and others paid no attention. It's the same way in every walk of life, in everything.

Q: Were there any cases of deliberate disrespect?

Mr. Sublett: I never saw any, never, never did, never had

any sour experience whatsoever.

Q: Did you find that a satisfying job, even though it wasn't what you really wanted?

Mr. Sublett: It was satisfying, because I knew that was my assignment. That's what they gave me to do, and that's what I was going to do. And I anticipated that they would have something else for me a little later. And they did. My next move was to San Francisco Bay area. I went aboard a converted yacht, pleasure yacht. It was a YP, which was yard patrol. So I'd patrol all around the San Francisco Bay area. When the submarines were out on dummy torpedo runs, I'd patrol the area. I was the skipper of this one.

Q: How did you get made the skipper rather than Martin?

Mr. Sublett: We alternated. On his days, he was the skipper. If I was on, I was skipper--port side, starboard side crews.

Q: I think he remembers you as being the skipper, and he worked for you.

Mr. Sublett: Maybe that was it, too. Maybe that was it. I think the other thing was on the oiler we were on later

Sublett #2 - 152

together. But I was the officer in charge. But I don't know how that came about either.

But our duty was to patrol the San Francisco Bay area within the Golden Gate limits. And occasionally we'd take pleasure cruises up and down the Bay.

Q: Not for your pleasure.

Mr. Sublett: Not for my pleasure. Maybe for the pleasure of a boat load of nurses, or WAVES, or somebody who had just gotten in the Navy and had to be familiarized with what a boat was like, or something like that.* I've got to call it a boat; it wasn't a ship.

Q: Did it really need two officers?

Mr. Sublett: No, and that's just another indication that they didn't know what to do with us.

Q: Did it need one officer?

Mr. Sublett: It did not. A first-class boatswain's mate could have done the job. Absolutely. I mean, we knew the rules of the road. That's all that was necessary. Know

---
*WAVES was an acronym for Women Accepted for Voluntary Emergency Service. Women were essentially a novelty in the Navy at that time; none except nurses were eligible for sea duty.

how to follow the channels, and how to acknowledge signals; to enter the Bay and go out and so forth, get permission to. And how to dock the ship, which was nothing rough--it was easy to do that without banging up a pier. The YP had a good engine crew.

Q: Was it a make-work kind of assignment, do you believe?

Mr. Sublett: I believe that, yes. Definitely.

Q: Did you find it more enjoyable than Hampton in that you at least you got to be out on the water?

Mr. Sublett: That part I enjoyed, yes. I did enjoy that a lot. And I could go fishing, too, at the same time. I mean, that was a lot of fun. I caught a lot of fish out there at Treasure Island, and that's where I tied up at the dock.

Q: Did you have some sort of living arrangement at Treasure Island?

Mr. Sublett: Not at Treasure Island. I lived in town. We had to provide our own quarters. We were given quarters allowance and subsistence. I found a rooming house over in

Sublett #2 - 154

Berkeley, a family that had a room that I could stay at. An old retired navy chief had a home and I was welcome to live there. So I paid rent to stay there.

Q: Were there navy quarters on Treasure Island?

Mr. Sublett: Yes.

Q: But you weren't welcome?

Mr. Sublett: But not for us. Exactly. BOQ?* Sure there was for navy nurses and the line officers.

Q: Did you get any guidance at any point about officers' clubs, and whether you could or couldn't go to them?

Mr. Sublett: No. I never attempted to go to an officers' club until I got out to the Pacific anyway. I wasn't a drinker, so I didn't know what else they did there. I didn't bother to go or try to go. I inquired about it. Then I had some old yarns from this Navy chief--I've forgotten what capacity he was--whether he was a cook at that time or just a plain steward's mate. But he was a chief. He had been in for 15-20 years. So he had a lot of negatives about the thing, because he didn't know any

---
*BOQ--bachelor officers' quarters.

Sublett #2 - 155

better. I mean, negatives about what to do and what you couldn't do.

Q: Well, you probably had more opportunity to encounter enlisted men in San Francisco than you had at Hampton.

Mr. Sublett: Sure did. I saw a lot of them full of wine lying in the streets. And I saw some that were seeking culture and some who were looking for good, clean fun.

By the way, I was offered a job after I came out of the Navy by the mayor of San Francisco. I've forgotten his name now, but at that time he was the mayor and said that if I wanted to make a home there, I was welcome to, and he'd find a position for me. I don't know what capacity.

Q: How did you come in contact with him?

Mr. Sublett: I don't remember that, but I used to go up to the courthouse. I used to go to Fisherman's Wharf; I used to go to Chinatown; I used to go to a lot of places there, just to look and learn. There were a few of us used to do that. I used to associate with enlisted men, by the way. There were not any more black officers around there to associate with.

Q: That's one of the usual prohibitions for an officer,

Sublett #2 - 156

against fraternizing.

Mr. Sublett: That's right, too. Fraternizing was forbidden, but what are you going to do when you're one and only one?

I've forgotten now how I met the mayor, but he was very congenial and friendly. Evidently, he made his point to meet me.

Q: That's a good sign.

Mr. Sublett: Yes, it was.

Q: Were there any racial restrictions on where you could go or what you could do?

Mr. Sublett: No, no. I didn't run into that.

Q: One of the early things that happened on board the vessel, as Mr. Martin told me, was that the white crew members were sent elsewhere.

Mr. Sublett: I thought I had a good crew--real good, as a matter of fact. And Martin remembers something that I don't know.

Sublett #2 - 157

Q: Well, what he remembers is that they were replaced by black men so that whites would not work for a black officer.

Mr. Sublett: I don't know if that was the reason or not. They might have been preparing the black kids to learn what things to do aboard a small boat with the future idea of putting us all on the Mason, as they did.* That's what I thought they were building to. I think I mentioned before we had a mixed crew on board that patrol craft. But for some reason they did ship them out, but I might have assumed it was routine.

Q: Did any of the white sailors express hesitation or resentment at serving with you?

Mr. Sublett: No, I didn't get any kickbacks at all or resentment of any kind.

Q: Did you get any indications in the other direction, people who were glad to serve under you?

Mr. Sublett: I did. From my engine room crew I did get

---

*The USS Mason (DE-529), a destroyer escort, was commissioned 20 March 1944 with a crew that comprised black enlisted personnel and white officers. James Hair, a member of the Golden Thirteen, became the Mason's first black officer.

Sublett #2 - 158

some indication of happiness and proudness to be in the service with me. Very favorable.

Q: Was the oiler a better assignment for you?

Mr. Sublett: It was more responsibility. Yes, it was a better assignment.

Q: It was a real job, too.

Mr. Sublett: It was a job. Handling an oiler is a challenge. You go to a loading dock at one of the oil refineries to take on a load; your tanker is empty. Currents are fast, the wind is strong, and it can be a problem. Many ship handlers have crashed the docks doing that. I had a commendation from the port director after a few months for my very good handling of that oiler. I could lay it up there easily, take a load, go out. Loaded or unloaded, I had very good capability. I had a good engine crew, a good helmsman. It was beautiful.

Q: Was this something you enjoyed doing?

Mr. Sublett: I liked that. I liked that a lot. And you'd come alongside a battlewagon or an aircraft carrier, and you'd lay up gently and that's seamanship and good ship handling. And I liked that very much. It was a challenge, because if you go barging into a newly painted ship, you've got trouble, I'm sure. So I liked that duty very, very much. That was the nearest thing to being Navy that I encountered during the time I served.

Q: Well, that's the kind of thing you went into the Navy for.

Mr. Sublett: That's what I wanted. Yes. Exactly it.

Q: Could you have happily continued to do that for a while longer?

Mr. Sublett: Oh, I would love to have. Sure. And I had a good crew. I had a signalman who was sharp. I mean, we'd answer signals. You were challenged each time you approached Treasure Island from out of the Bay or coming down the channel, and you would have to respond. I had a terrific signalman who could carry out the orders, and the engine room crew were excellent. And the deck crew could handle the hoses. Some hoses could beat heck out of you. You'd lose them on the booms when they're not very confident. You can have oil spills. We had a good clean oiler and a good clean crew--real terrific.

I had a warrant officer with me, too, on that oiler.

Sublett #2 - 160

His name was Louis Johnson, and he was from Albany, New York.

Q: Johnson must have been one of the very first black warrant officers after Lear then.

Mr. Sublett: He was. He came in as a warrant, and he served with me at Treasure Island. I'll never forget him, because he used to smoke a lot, and he had a cigarette holder, and I thought that was weird. At any rate, he was a good man and I don't know what his responsibilities were, because what was there for him to do as a second officer? We played pinochle a lot aboard the craft while in port.

Q: How large was the crew on the oiler?

Mr. Sublett: I have no idea right now, but a good crew.

Q: Were there any disciplinary problems?

Mr. Sublett: Aboard there I did not have any disciplinary problems, no. I think my first experience with disciplinary problems was at Hampton. A couple of guys didn't want to be in the Navy, and they goofed up. But after that, it was out in Eniwetok. Some more brig busters. They found it more comfortable in the brig than they did in their own barracks, I guess. They were trying to get out of the Navy. That was the whole story. And they didn't do any criminal things, just things that were not conducive to what they were supposed to be doing.

But after the oiler assignment I went to Great Lakes for a VD class. It lasted two weeks, and I asked for an extension because I was home. And then I went back to Hampton and taught some of the young people who were starting out on liberty about the importance of cleanliness and protection and that sort of thing when they went ashore. It was quite beneficial for a lot of them, but some would not heed the precaution, as always.

Q: Did they have movies as part of this training?

Mr. Sublett: For me, instructional movies, yes, but when I presented it, it had to be just lecture. And that was the extent of my training to them, just lecture.

Q: I remember when I was in OCS they had these movies that were really comical, because the drama part of it was so amateurish.* A destroyer escort was incapacitated by VD, so they couldn't operate effectively against the Japanese.

Mr. Sublett: Right.

---
*OCS--officer candidate school.

Sublett #2 - 162

Q: So we called those the rotten-crotch movies.

Mr. Sublett: (Laughter) Very fitting, very fitting. And some of those guys wished they had not gotten rotten crotch.

Q: So then you went overseas. Was that something you were happy to do?

Mr. Sublett: Well, at first the thought of going was beautiful. But as I got to Pearl Harbor, I thought I was going to get on something bigger than what I was on. So at Pearl Harbor, I think it must have been an officers' pool at Manana Barracks. That's when I saw the first black doctors and dentists. They were waiting also for assignment.

So I stayed there for a couple of weeks, I guess. That's when I met Nelson again, and we shipped out together from there to Eniwetok. We went to a logistics support company. And the officer in charge there was Lieutenant Reed. I think he was from somewhere in Pennsylvania, a white officer. That's when I met Sidney Smith, who was another black warrant officer. And I don't know when Martin came there. He might have gotten there the same time as Nelson and myself.

Sublett #2 - 163

Q: He's in some of those pictures you showed me.

Mr. Sublett: Right. I've forgotten whether he went with us; I don't recall seeing Martin in Pearl Harbor so he might have come a little bit after, and Sidney Smith, also.

Q: And what was your job there?

Mr. Sublett: The logistic support company was loading or unloading transport ships, supervising the loading and unloading. That's what we had the crews there for.

Q: Was this largely stevedore-type work?

Mr. Sublett: It was stevedore-type work, yes.

We had a recreational setup there. Martin was in charge of that. And Sidney Smith, who was a machinist, was in charge of converting sea water to fresh water. And I was the exec. Like I said, Lieutenant Reed was officer in charge. And we were just supervising the loading and unloading of these transports. There was a beautiful horseshoe-shaped lagoon in Eniwetok there in the Marshall Islands; it was real nice. Actually, they were setting up for and preparing for the invasion of Japan. There were more ships there than I'd ever seen before, all types.

Q: Probably the sort of thing that would make you envious.

Mr. Sublett: Absolutely. I wanted to go. But there was nothing other than that. I don't remember what we did with the material that was loaded and unloaded and transported from one ship to another. I think some of the guys would bring ashore some of the goodies that we'd have. Like I said before, men would build a big bonfire and they'd have a roast out and invite the officers in. The runway had already been built by the Seabees prior to our arrival. It was small island, about three miles long or something like that, and they had an airstrip on there; that was the biggest thing there.

Q: What was the climate like?

Mr. Sublett: The climate was perfect, absolutely perfect. Of course, it is all sand. And beautiful, tropical air. I could go swimming in 20 feet of water and it looked like it was just about ten feet. It was that clear. It was beautiful down there.

And we used to go and collect seashells when we were off duty. Nelson and I did that a lot. Eniwetok had an officers' club. That's the first officers' club that I ventured into. I did not have any problem whatsoever. I went there, purchased my liquor, and sold it. I still did not drink. I've forgotten what I went through to sell it, but I bought it for a buck-and-a-half a fifth, I guess, or something like that. And it would go for $18.00 or $20.00 or better. A dirty shame to take advantage of people like that, but I sent the money home.

Q: How large a group was this that you and Reed were in charge of?

Mr. Sublett: Oh, I've forgotten now. There must have been a couple hundred or better in that outfit.

Q: All black.

Mr. Sublett: Yes, they were all black. The Seabees had built the airstrip, and there were a few of them left. There were a few Marines. There were some white officers in other outfits. There were other logistic support outfits, white. And ours was the only black, I think. And so there had to be over 200 men in that one.

Q: I can imagine you had quite a load of paperwork with that number of people.

Mr. Sublett: Oh, it was plenty. For four officers, there

was quite a bit to do.

Q: What was Nelson's role?

Mr. Sublett: He was supply officer and personnel officer. And there we had to set up captain's mast a few times.

Q: Was Nelson as flamboyant there as he was back at Great Lakes?

Mr. Sublett: As much as he could be, but it was limited because of there was no one to perform for. Like I said, he and I had a lot of fun in the ocean. He liked the water, too. But he loved these little shells. I still have a lot of those seashells, cat's eyes and all, other pretty little things we used for trinkets. We used to make the bracelets, necklaces. He was very adept at that. He liked it a lot. And we'd go to the officers' club and we'd talk. There were outdoor movies. That was the recreation. And there was a nurses' quarters nearby; they had nurses there. It was a collecting station or place for further movement to Japan, and that's what they were preparing for.

Q: While we changed tapes, you said that on Eniwetok Nelson had a system of speaking to you there that you found amusing.

Mr. Sublett: Oh, that was in reference to office intercommunication between executives, like big corporations, like the president or vice presidents would address each other with their first two initials, like "D.D., what's up for today?" "This is F.E. calling. Do you have time for golf this evening?" or something of that nature. So we played with that and had a lot of fun with it, joking.

Q: This is still another example where he tried to create an important situation.

Mr. Sublett: Yes, just transpose it to another situation. High executive type communicating with a peer.

Q: Well, it sounds like you reciprocated.

Mr. Sublett: Oh, yes, it was a familiar type of thing that I had heard. So it fit right in for fun.

Q: So if he wanted to go out to chow that night, he'd say, "F.E., this is D.D."

Mr. Sublett: Exactly. "D.D., what's up? This is F.E.

calling responding to your request to go to chow. Let's do it."

Yes, those were quite fun days.

Q: Were there segregated living arrangements there at Eniwetok?

Mr. Sublett: Well, in a sense, because our logistic support outfit was all black. All the officers slept in the headquarters and ate together. As I said, Lieutenant George Reed was white. I used white, but I should say Caucasian, maybe. Reed was one gentleman. He was very warm and congenial, and he was no different from the rest of us. We were all officers, as it should be, without regard to color or race or anything like that. We all worked together.

Q: You showed me some pictures in which Nelson had a bandage on his leg.

Mr. Sublett: Well, that was a coral cut. We were out wading around, or swimming--one or the other. And he got this cut on his shin. It took a long, long time to heal. I don't remember ever seeing it heal before I left. He was still there when I left. By the time of the bombing of Hiroshima and then the announcing of the end of the war, I

Sublett #2 - 169

had accumulated enough points to come home. I wanted to stay in, but my mother-in-law had anxiety problems about me coming home to take care of my family.

Anyway, Nelson stayed. He had also enough points, but he stayed in. I was a lieutenant jaygee at the time, and was offered another half stripe to stay. And I would love to have stayed. I wish today that I had, but Nelson stayed in, and he was still ailing with that mark or scratch or scar on his leg when I last saw him at Eniwetok.

Q: Was there something about coral that made it difficult to heal?

Mr. Sublett: Coral cuts are very difficult to heal, anyway. And I don't know whether there was any other particular reason that his was slower to heal than normal.

No, he was not as flamboyant there, but he was very anxious to rule the roost, so to speak. He would like to have been the commanding officer in that particular outfit.

Q: Did you ride over and back in navy transports?

Mr. Sublett: I went to Eniwetok on a navy transport. When I returned to Pearl Harbor from Eniwetok, I was on a PC. And that PC bounced, and rolled, and pitched, and that was the fiercest boat ride that I ever had. It took five days

Sublett #2 - 170

or something like that to go back to Pearl. And it was real, real stormy. As a matter of fact, we lost a man overboard. It was a white kid who was returning to the States on points to be discharged from the service. And it was a sad occasion. I've forgotten where he came from, because he came from another island. There were a bunch of islands out in that area.

Q: You showed me some orders that you had ridden from the West Coast out to Hawaii in the USS <u>Joseph Dickman</u>, APA-13.

Mr. Sublett: APA-13.

Q: Was there any discrimination for you in these transports when you made these rides?

Mr. Sublett: Not particularly. I boarded that particular transport in San Francisco. There were navy personnel on board; there were Marines aboard; and, if I'm not mistaken, there were Army aboard. Each group was designated to certain areas, and where to bunk and where to chow. And there were no problems whatsoever. I never saw any. Nothing but friendship. There was a war going on, and they didn't know where they were going, so half of them were afraid, too, and didn't know what the future might bring for them. So they were not thinking too much of color

Sublett #2 - 171

problems at that time, as far as I could tell. I didn't notice any problem at all.

Q: Were there any events of note when you got back to the States, before you were discharged?

Mr. Sublett: No, not particularly. When I came to Great Lakes, one of the first persons that I saw at Great Lakes was a young lady whom I had gone through grade school and high school with, and who I just recently saw at my 50th class reunion. She was a WAVE and working on the main side in the separation center.

Nothing eventful occurred that time. I was assigned to Naval Reserve for ten years, and that was about it. That was in late '45, and then in '46 I was terminated.

Q: Did you give any thought of going back to college at that point?

Mr. Sublett: I wanted to, but then I had to go out and make a living, and so I went to work instead. I went right back to the job that I had been working during summers when going to school. I went back to the Buick dealership, and I started out as a mechanic, body repairman, worked in the parts department. And then I went to service writer. I worked there from '46 until '51 as assistant service manager. Then I went to another dealership in Buick, in Highland Park, and I worked there for 30 years, so that's the only type of job I've ever had. I was service manager there for 30 years, and really retired in '80 and went to a new career, modeling.

Q: Was the GI Bill available for you when the war ended?

Mr. Sublett: I don't know how soon after the war ended that the GI Bill was available, but it was at one point.* And I thought many times of going for it, but then I thought I'd better go to work. Maybe I made a mistake there, too. I should have given myself another year and completed my education.

Then I became the first black service manager for Buick in the Chicago metropolitan area. It was a good experience, too. Being in a job that involves serving the public can be a problem for people. But it all depends, again, on attitude. I came out of that unscathed, no ulcers and whatnot.

Q: Did your wife have any feelings on this question of going to a job or college at that point?

---

*The GI Bill of Rights, or Servicemen's Adjustment Act of 1944, was signed into law by President Franklin D. Roosevelt on 22 June 1944. It provided educational support and other benefits for all veterans discharged with six or more months of service after 16 September 1940.

Sublett #2 - 173

Mr. Sublett: Actually, she had no part to play in it, not at all. No, we were not too congenial at that time. It was not a happy marriage; I'll put it that way. She didn't have any bearing on it; her thoughts weren't involved in anything that I had to do. I knew my responsibilities, and that was the extent of it. We finally parted.

Q: The big thing for her family was the question of you coming home rather than staying in the Navy.

Mr. Sublett: Yes, they thought it might help for her to slow down a bit. She was running around, into situations that she shouldn't have been in and, therefore, they thought my presence would help. It helped for a little while. But it was just not to be for us, so it finally ended.

Q: You showed me a letter that you got in 1949 from the Navy inquiring about you coming back in as a recruiter to "encourage colored boys" to come in. Why did you not pursue that one?

Mr. Sublett: Again, I wanted to. That was my last opportunity, actually, to get back and do what I really wanted to do. But I had a young family growing up, and I felt my responsibilities were with them. And that's why I didn't go. And I truly wish today that I had gone back into the Navy and served. But it's history.

Q: It's the benefit of hindsight now, too.

Mr. Sublett: Right. Exactly.

Q: What has become of your children? What sorts of things have they gone into?

Mr. Sublett: I have two sons, and I have two daughters. My older son Frank has worked in laboratories, like Baxter Laboratories. And then they cut back and he's been let go, and then they rehired him again, and they cut back again, and let him go. He did not have a diploma. That made the difference in his career, although I don't know how he got into the lab work to begin with. He's a real intelligent youngster.

And my younger son Michael is a guitarist. So he's into music groups playing and singing and that sort.

My older daughter Rosanne right now is going to law school. She's studying criminal law in Michigan. And my younger daughter Nicole was married and just being a house mother. My older boy was quite good at ice skating. He was a member of the Northbrook Skating Club, and did well

Sublett #2 - 175

in silver skates, and state meets, and that sort of thing. That was in his growing years.

My younger boy was a good basketball player, still is, and hockey. He was a terrific hockey player. And my older daughter likes to dance. But, anyway, she's the smart one of the group.

Q: Do they have a sense of appreciation for your place in history?

Mr. Sublett: The children do. Definitely. It took a while for them to realize, too. I mean, they grew up here, as I did. Again, maybe that's why I raised my family here, because I wanted them to have the same opportunities that I had. And a good environment and the good schools, and so forth. And it was a while, because they just took it for granted that what I did was okay. But I think some of their school chums just made them realize what it amounted to. They'd seen articles in history books at school regarding my accomplishments. So they have been very aware of it and they've seen instances on television, heard it on radio, and seen in periodicals what I'd done. So they're quite proud.

Q: Well, I think that probably helps build their sense of racial pride, also.

Mr. Sublett: Well, on that racial business, they may be now as adults, but they grew up here in the same atmosphere, same environment. And they were not aware of any of that garbage with race until they became older. They dated who they wanted to, and that was it.

Q: It's not something you made an issue of.

Mr. Sublett: No, no, no. I've never made any issue of that around my home at all, ever. People are people, and no matter what they look like or where they came from. Respect people as people. They're human. And that's it. So I think they, just by growing up in the atmosphere of not having any negatives about anybody, it just hasn't dawned on them that there was a situation that they had to be told about.

Live and let live; learn what you can. They've all done pretty well.

Q: What do you recall about that process of coming back together again with the rest of the Golden Thirteen? How did that come about?

Mr. Sublett: Oh, I think the first notice I got on that came early in 1977. Would I be interested in meeting with my old shipmates again, or something to that effect, in a

Sublett #2 - 177

reunion in 1977? And I responded, "Yes," and anxiously looked forwarded to seeing the old fellows that I hadn't seen since 1945 some of them, and some 1944.

Q: Who was the instigator of that?

Mr. Sublett: I would have to go on reference only and not from definite, direct information. I think Nelson was involved greatly in achieving the possibility of us meeting again, because he had stayed in the service and achieved the rank of lieutenant commander. I guess he had a lot of interest in our well-being and wanted to regroup again. I think that's how it was started. And whoever his contacts were were agreeable enough to carry it out for us. I don't know who assisted in it, or who really pushed it through, but it worked through the Navy Recruiting Command, and that's how we came together again. We were all invited to Berkeley, California, in '77, in July. And that was a real regrouping.

Q: What specific memories do you have of that occasion?

Mr. Sublett: How happy we were all to see each other again. We reminisced about our school days at Great Lakes. We talked about how we had changed and what each one of us had gone through through the years since we had last seen

Sublett #2 - 178

each other.

It was a real experience--a real joy to see them all again.

Q: At that time, did you envision this would become an annual thing?

Mr. Sublett: No, I really didn't. I didn't think any more of it until the following year when it was suggested that we meet again in order to help in some fashion the recruiting command, and getting youngsters to be involved with the Navy. The idea was that the opportunities were so different now than they were then that we thought we might be able to help youngsters realize that the opportunity is here and to take advantage of it--for school, for learning, for a career, and that sort. I was surprised and happy that it continued, and it has. Fortunately, it's done some good for the Navy because it has continued. And that's what it's all about for Navy recruitment and retention.

Q: Was it initially sort of a private venture and then the Navy got involved in sponsoring it?

Mr. Sublett: No, evidently, the Navy saw at the beginning that it was a thing that would achieve the goal of getting minorities interested in the Navy. It was not privately sponsored at all. It all came about through the Navy Recruiting Command. Since that time we've tried in every way to get youngsters who were qualified to get into the service and take advantage of all these opportunities that are available.

It hasn't been an individual effort. It has been a group effort on all our parts. Some of us live in different locations and have different opportunities to meet these people who are available for the service, and therefore, pass on the information that they need.

Q: Are there any specific things that you've been involved in that have been very satisfying in that regard?

Mr. Sublett: Not one incident. I mean, I've passed the word. I've talked. I do not have the minority youngsters in this area whom I can talk with, because there are none. Most of the kids in this area can afford to go to college, and do go to college. I've talked to a couple of them, however. There has been one young man from this area who went to Annapolis. I think he dropped out, but he did go. And I wish he had stayed in, but nothing I can do about that.

But not one particular person that I have been able to put into the service.

Sublett #2 - 180

Q: Is the visit to the Kidd the highlight of the reunions?

Mr. Sublett: The visit to the Kidd was really a highlight. It was an explosive situation to see such a great change in the facilities of today's Navy and yesterday's Navy. I mean, the weaponry, the construction, the equipment. It's hard to believe that it's so changed for the better. Today's Navy requires a young man to be well versed in mathematics, in all the hard sciences, and electronics that are available in order to be a good navy man.

Whereas, in the old days, there used to be "pass the ammunition" idea. Those days are gone. A man has to be really qualified to operate satisfactorily in this Navy. But it's there for you. All you have to do is work for it. It's there.

Q: After 38 years they finally let you aboard a warship.

Mr. Sublett: Yes, that's exactly right. And that was a real thrill. I enjoyed that greatly. The power, for one thing, was something that you read about, but rarely get the chance to experience. And the electronic boards, the printouts. It's just amazing how science has changed everything, all the workings of the ship, maneuvers.

Q: What do you remember about the return of Hair?

Sublett #2 - 181

Mr. Sublett: Oh, the return of Hair was like the arrival of a new baby. Except it was something we hadn't expected. And when we did get the notice that he was coming aboard, it was new all over again. How and why had he been away from us so long? We don't know today. But it was a real great inspiration to have him join us again. He was a good person to have there.

Q: Two members of your group have died since the reunions began, Nelson and Baugh. What observances were made on those occasions?

Mr. Sublett: We missed Nelson a lot, because, as I said, I think Nelson was a big help in getting our group back together. He'd done a heck of a lot for us as a group. He was pure Navy, all the way Navy, and he wanted us to share it with him. He thought it would be nothing better than to get us all back together again.

Baugh was a hard worker. He brought a lot of youngsters into the Navy. He was very active, as a matter of fact, in the Boston area with the youth. And he had very good rapport with the recruiting district up there. He did a lot of work individually in getting new members into the Navy. He loved the Navy also, was thoroughly for it. They're really missed for their contribution.

Q: Did the group send a representative to the funerals?

Mr. Sublett: John Reagan went to Nelson's funeral and represented our group. I've forgotten who went to Baugh's funeral, but someone from our group represented us there, as it should have been. And those were two hard-working men that are still greatly missed for their efforts in keeping us together. And the Navy misses them, too, for their contributions.

Q: I gather that people liked Nelson despite his flamboyant, ostentatious ways.

Mr. Sublett: People loved Nelson. He was flamboyant, wild, and sometimes crude, maybe, but everybody loved him. I mean, you could be angry with him in one minute, and the next minute you just loved him, just for his misdemeanors and how sneakily he got out of them with a big laugh. He thought he was funny. But you didn't get angry enough with him to battle him, let's say. A lot of times there was sympathy too. But, nevertheless, he brought a lot of cheer.

Q: What sort of sympathy, for what?

Sublett #2 - 183

Mr. Sublett: For being stupid. That's exactly what sometimes the things were. But he came out of it unscathed.

Q: How would he sneak out of a misdemeanor?

Mr. Sublett: Well, he'd come up with some sort of a weak joke, and then you forgot the previous statement. He was clever at that. I don't know how he came about that. It might have been natural, because I understand he was a teacher at one time. I can't imagine him being serious in a classroom for any length of time and not pass an off-color quip of some sort, because he was full of them.

Q: Yes, but it's hard to imagine a better setting for Nelson than a classroom because he was the center of attention.

Mr. Sublett: Well, he liked that. Oh, yes, the center of attention: "This is me. I'm here. Focus everything on me." He lived for that; indeed, he did. He had a flair for being the idol of attention.

Q: What would you classify as one of his misdemeanors?

Mr. Sublett: Oh, gosh, I can't tell you now. I've been

trying to think of some of his silly little jokes. There was one in particular about the mouse and the elephant. But it was off-color and I wish I could think of it, because it was funny.

The misdemeanor that I hear about was when he was stationed at Great Lakes and very arrogantly riding around in his little convertible automobile and defying the orders of the commanding officer in some direction that the commanding officer didn't like. And I don't know what it was. But he defied it day after day after day, and he got away with it. I don't know what it was he had about him, but, like with our group, he'd do something, and then maybe somebody would say, "What are you doing that for?" or worse terms than that, of course. And then the next, he's laughing, which would forgive him, so to speak.

Q: Have you been involved in any civic activities in the community?

Mr. Sublett: No, I have not. After my wife and I broke up, I had a full-time job of raising three kids and working, maintaining a home and that sort of thing, so I had very little time for anything like that. When I worked for an auto dealership, I'd open the doors at 7:30 in the morning. Sometimes I didn't get home until dinner time, so I had to find time for all the house chores and yard chores, and all that sort of thing, and help with study. I got involved in whatever the kids required and sometimes taking them into Cub Scout meetings or Boy Scout meetings, or wherever the things they had to do. And I had some help occasionally from a neighbor, but, no, I've not been active in civic activities.

Q: That didn't leave much time for you.

Mr. Sublett: No, I had little time. There have been years that I did not take a vacation during summer, because I had obligations that I had to keep up with. I'm sorry I did that, though. I think vacations would have been a lot better for me than grinding away steadily. I didn't gain that much by that. I wouldn't recommend that at all.

Q: At what point did you get remarried?

Mr. Sublett: I married Frances in '64. And I had a little girl by her. And that didn't work out after about five years. They now live in Detroit, and my little daughter is married and has her own family. Then I was a bachelor a long time from then until '75, when I married Karen. Anyway, I'm happy now.

Q: This one is for keeps.

Sublett #2 - 186

Mr. Sublett: I'm happy now. Indeed.

Q: Well, we haven't talked about your modeling career. You told me last time how it came about, but I'd be interested in some of the specifics of the work with the agency and some of the interesting jobs you've had.

Mr. Sublett: Most of my work has been print work. I have done some small movie bits. I've been extras in movies. I've done in-house industrial films as a judge, as a doctor, as a pharmacist. I've done work for Pillsbury for covers on magazines and flyers--Illinois Bell Telephone, Sears Roebuck, a lot of banks, and for pharmaceutical companies, a lot of print work for them. I have been a process server. And it's been very interesting. I like it. You meet different people, and it's fun doing it. I've done robes for cap and gown people.

I do not get regular work. I am associated with one agency, and they know my capabilities. They have my picture; they pass it around. There are several catalogs that my picture appears in. They know all my qualifications, and it isn't often they have a call for a person of my caliber or my age group and that. Even youngsters don't work steadily at it, unless you are a fashion model, which I am not. And I find it really interesting, and it's something I can do for a long time, hopefully.

Q: You said that one of the handicaps you have is that you're considered by some people too young-looking to be a grandfather.

Mr. Sublett: Well, I'm often told that I don't look like I am a grandfather. I have 12 grandchildren, and I have three great-grandchildren at this point. And that's true. I have some gray hair, but when they think of grandfathers, they don't realize that there are young-looking grandfathers. They may picture a white-haired man stooped over, and what-not, maybe not walking, or limping with arthritis. I have it, but I don't limp from it too often. So I've been fortunate in that way. I can play a younger man's role, too, as a vice president of a corporation, or a board member of some corporation or bank. I have played grandfather roles sometimes. As a matter of fact, I was with a girl in one ad, teaching her how to be involved with a computer. As a matter of fact, that's the last thing I had. I've done some national commercials on television. That has been fun.

Q: One you were telling me about, last time when the recorder wasn't running, was the Bud Light commercial.

Sublett #2 - 188

What do you remember about that?

Mr. Sublett: Oh, that Bud Light commercial was filmed at Comiskey Park, the baseball park where the White Sox play. And I'm trying to think of the exact details about it, but I remember sitting there and I think applauding for something that occurred at the park. And the model next to me was saying something about Bud Light. That was a few years ago.

Q: As I remember the commercial, the scoreboard erupted in fireworks, and the man beside you said, "No, I asked for a Bud Light."

Mr. Sublett: That's exactly what it was. He asked for a Bud Light and the scoreboard exploded. All the fireworks went off and lit up like you've never seen before, and somebody was real confused. He asked for a Bud Light, and they just thought he wanted a light, so gave him plenty of light.* That was funny.

Q: How long does it take to film a commercial that shows on the screen for, maybe, ten or 15 seconds?

---
*This was one of many in an advertising campaign. The typical scenario called for the delivery of some zany or spectacular display of lights, to which a person in the commercial would respond, "But I asked for a Bud Light." The thrust of the campaign was to get customers to ask specifically for a Bud Light, not just for a light beer.

Mr. Sublett: Well, sometimes it takes four hours, sometimes longer. It depends on the setting. I know I did one for which I had to go back for three auditions. I was selected on the first audition, but they had to go through seven or eight other models in order to select the right one they wanted to work with me. So that, I would say, entailed an hour each there, and then the actual filming of it was about three hours. Sometimes they're lengthy. I did one print job that took four hours, and that was just for my hands. For Pillsbury I did an ad that just filmed my hands opening a biscuit. I did another with an orange between my two hands; that was a face-on job. That took a couple of hours, and it was just a simple setting.

The most tedious was for caps and gowns. These particular gowns were for priests and reverends. And each pleat had to be just so, each fold had to be just so, and not a speck of lint. And that was the most tedious job that I've done. And that took some time.

I look forward to doing that again. Actually, I will do it next year; every other year I get called for that job. I like it. It's from a place down near the University of Illinois, down in Urbana. I look forward for that one, because they'll call me back each time they do it.

Sublett #2 - 190

Q: Do you get speaking roles in any of these?

Mr. Sublett: I've only had short scripts in all of these, any of these.

Q: What is the role of the cattle call in this business?

Mr. Sublett: A cattle call, they'll say, "Go to an audition for such-and-such a company." Well, you go there and you find a full range of ages. And that makes too many. What they want is either a young man or an older man. And that should be categorized when you go on the audition--a young person or an older person. And that's too big a range for anyone to cover. And so it's just a waste of time, actually. And that costs money to go on an audition. You don't get paid for that. And you have to take various wardrobes with you, too, on some calls. Some, they supply wardrobes, but not always.

Q: Are any of these that you really feel were the most enjoyable?

Mr. Sublett: I have fun with all of them. I've done one for a cigarette. I don't smoke, but it has an adjustable tip on it to adjust the amount of nicotine that you want

Sublett #2 - 191

from that cigarette. That was for Philip Morris.

I don't know what I can say is the most fun. One that was rather loose was for the van line. There were a bunch of us on that. We're all standing out on a huge lawn out here in Barrington and looking toward this huge, big Allied Van Lines truck, and standing just as casual as can be. It took a couple of hours to shoot that simple little thing. There probably have been some others that have been fun. But they're all enjoyable, though. You meet a lot of people on them. And sometimes you meet the same people. I've worked with some people on a number of occasions, and each time it's fun.

Q: Well, I'm sure the public image of modeling is that of glamorous occupation.

Mr. Sublett: Well, yes, they see the fashion models, and they think that all of the models fit that same role. But that isn't so. They don't take models for handsome looks, particularly, anymore. They take for specifics like maybe your nose, maybe your hair, maybe your hands, maybe your nails, how you smile or something like that. You may be fat, you may be thin. You may have a beard that looks unfavorable mostly--you wouldn't anticipate just an ordinary old gray beard guy, but it's what they want for the shot. And it isn't the immaculately dressed young lady or young man anymore. It's a variety and good, good range.

Q: James Hair told me that he was hired for a modeling job during World War II. Until it came time to discuss backgrounds and he revealed he'd been to Bethune-Cookman, and that was the end of his modeling.

Mr. Sublett: That killed that. Well, anyone black at that time was out of the picture.

Q: Literally.

Mr. Sublett: Indeed. Absolutely.

Q: What other sorts of occupations have you been involved in in recent years?

Mr. Sublett: Well, now and for the last eight years or so since retirement from the auto industry, I have a home security business. I have a few homes that I take care of year-round. And some I take care of while people are out of the country or out of the state for any length of time, whether vacations or what have you. And that is fun, too. It's not a laboring job, but there's a responsibility.

Q: It's obviously a testimony to your reliability as well.

Mr. Sublett: That's definitely true, because word of mouth goes, and so I can be trusted in that.

I recently had an offer to work as a bank vault attendant. I don't know what the title would be, and I don't know yet whether I'm going to engage in that or not. I've been thinking about it. There isn't much responsibility there. It's just a matter of escorting people to the safety deposit box and escorting them out.

Q: What sorts of things do you do for enjoyment these days?

Mr. Sublett: Oh, I go boating. I have a couple of friends. As a matter of fact, this coming Sunday we're going sailboating. We're invited to a neighbor with a pretty big sailboat, and we'll go out, and we'll see the air show from Lake Michigan. And another doctor friend who has a boat and who thinks that because I was in the Navy and handled small craft that I'm the best. And I still handle it pretty well; we go out on Fox Lake and that area.

I have done a little bowling, but not in the last few years.

And I have another friend who along with his dad and uncle own jointly a cabin cruiser. They berth that at Burnham Harbor in Chicago, and we go out on that occasionally.

We go out picnicking, or on cookouts with our friends, and we cook out here and invite a few friends over. Occasionally I go to a football game when I can. I take in one or two baseball games each summer. I have a very good friend who is part owner of the Chicago Bulls. So I take in a basketball game occasionally, gratis. And that's about it.

My kids don't come around often enough for me to toss a ball with them, so I'm lost in that area now. I take Karen out and we catch ball or toss a frisbee or something like that around.

I don't have golf clubs anymore. I have access to some, but it's too tough to get on the golf course anymore. It's so crowded. You get out early in the morning, and you can't get on.

I used to do a lot of fishing, as I told you before. But that's gotten to be so darn miserable because of the overcrowdedness, and also the polluted waters. It's terrible. I used to go up to Wisconsin every spring for the bass run. And I don't do that anymore, because it's not good eating anymore, good fishing. And it's overcrowded, also. I used to do a lot of hunting; I don't do that because you have to go too far away, and it isn't safe anymore.

So I have a lot to do here, like puttering in my

garden. I raise a vegetable garden every year. And Karen has some flowers, and I've got maintenance on the house to take care of and around the yard, which I enjoy. It's outside work. That's what I like most, the outdoors.

I walk a lot and ride my bike a lot. I belong to a health club. I go there and work out--on the Nautilus machines and the bicycles, and whatever, the rowing machines. I belong to a swim club. I haven't used it as much as I should have this year, but I'll get back to it.

Q: One of the themes that you've mentioned to me are the obligations of being a good citizen. What are your thoughts on that?

Mr. Sublett: Well, I think everybody has an opportunity to be a first-class citizen, and I think that comes first. We can gripe and groan about our personal problems, not having what you want in life. But you can do without and still be a first-class citizen by taking care of your own business, your own home, and your own surroundings. And not worrying too much about the other person, what he has or doesn't have. And by not bothering him and taking from him what belongs to him. This comes from lower class all the way up to the so-called higher class who has everything. I mean they're stealing, also. And they're not good citizens. So good, clean living, respecting each other as a person, and

Sublett #2 - 196

I think that makes a good citizen.

I think if you can help someone, help him. If you can't help him, leave him alone. But I think those are a couple of things that contribute to a real good citizen.

Q: Keeping informed and voting are a couple other obligations.

Mr. Sublett: Oh, that's definitely a must. I mean I've served on jury duty. I've voted each time that it's necessary and that sort of thing. And certainly those, I think, are the duties of any good citizen. Absolutely. You have your small say-so in the governing of your area, and your area includes the country.

Q: You've described a life that, for the most part, revolves around this community in Illinois. The biggest exception was your time in the Navy.

Mr. Sublett: That is true.

Q: How does that Navy experience fit in your overall life?

Mr. Sublett: Well, that overall experience taught me further, I'm sure, how to cope with people from other walks of life. Those who do not have the opportunities that I've had are still entitled to respect as human beings. And they are entitled to be treated as equals, regardless of what they look like, or what color they are. The Navy has also enlightened me on how to appreciate what is available to me. And I had an experience of travel in the Navy that I definitely would not have been afforded during those years. I've seen poverty, and I've seen wealth and had good times in those areas. And I can appreciate what people are doing in other parts of the world.

In the overall, the Navy contributed something to my adulthood that, except for my private life with my family, which had nothing to do with it really. It just wasn't there.

Q: My guess, also, is that by being such a contrast to how you spent most of the rest of your life, it's among the most memorable part of it.

Mr. Sublett: Well, definitely it's the most memorable. Looking back on it, it was the outstanding thing that happened to me in my lifetime.

And I'm happy that my mother is alive and could share that with me. Now last year, on June 6, there was a building dedicated to the Golden Thirteen up at Great Lakes, and my mother went with me; I took her to the dedication. And she was most proud, and I was proud to

Sublett #2 - 198

have her with me. Admiral Hazard was so very kind to my mother, and everyone else up there to comfort her and let her share in the proceedings.* And that was a big, big event in my life. So the Navy's still good to me.

Q: What else do you remember about that occasion?

Mr. Sublett: Well, the dedication of that building was a real tribute to our being the group that we are. Every sailor that goes through Great Lakes for recruiting goes through that particular building. And it's good to know that we are recognized and will be forever by each sailor who goes through there. He might not think so at the time, but then sometime he might be told how that came about. And it's great to know that this has happened and why. That's a big factor in respect for what we did and are still doing, because we push hard for the Navy.

Q: What is your role at the museum in connection with the building?

Mr. Sublett: Well, I have taken upon myself to keep in touch with the public relations people at Great Lakes to follow through on whatever memorabilia can be salvaged from our group, to be put on display and let it be known what we

---
*Rear Admiral Roberta L. Hazard, USN, Commander Naval Training Center, Great Lakes, Illinois.

did, and what we wore, and how we conducted ourselves when we were in the service actively.

Q: Your wife showed me a book that was put out on the 50th anniversary of Life magazine coming into being. Among the photos in that book was one of the Golden Thirteen, and it's interesting that that should be included.

Mr. Sublett: Well, fortunately, that was within the last 50 years, and they are regrouping all the main events that happened in that period, and we were fortunate to be a part of it. And they're reprinting it again. So often that comes about. And it's nice to know we have not been forgotten by not only the Navy but the media.

Q: Any final thoughts?

Mr. Sublett: Well, I would like to say that it's been a real, real pleasure to have you visit my home again. I thoroughly enjoyed it; the interview has been absolutely enjoyable. It brings back good memories also from your last visit, and also from our group of Navy people that I went through school with, our Golden Thirteen as a group. And it reminds me that there are greater things to come possibly from this interview. And I thoroughly appreciate your time.

Q: Well, it's a labor of love with me. I very much enjoy the associations I've had with members of the group. I feel it's an honor to have that association, and I'm very grateful for your contribution.

Mr. Sublett: Any time you're in this area, on Navy duty or not, you're welcome in my home at any time.

Q: Thank you very much.

Mr. Sublett: Thank you.

Index

to

Reminiscences

of

Mr. Frank E. Sublett, Jr.

Arbor, Jesse W.
    Golden Thirteen member who added humor to the officer training program in early 1944, 33; Navy recruiting work in recent years, 64

Armstrong, Commander Daniel W., USNR (USNA, 1915)
    Served as officer in charge of Camp Robert Smalls at Great Lakes, Illinois, during World War II, 27, 39, 115-116, 138

Army, U.S.
    Sponsored Citizens Military Training Camp at Fort Riley, Kansas, in the 1930s for the benefit of teenage boys, 12, 92-96

Army Air Forces, U.S.
    Sublett tried to become a pilot early in World War II, but no openings were available, 3, 10, 96

Barnes, Phillip G.
    Golden Thirteen member whose sister provided information from Washington, D.C., during the training period in early 1944, 25, 33-34

Barnes, Samuel E.
    Golden Thirteen member who went through the officer training program in early 1944, 34

Baugh, Dalton L.
    Golden Thirteen member who went through the officer training program in early 1944, 34, 181

Black Naval Officers
    Increased opportunities in recent years, 65-66
    See also Golden Thirteen

Boy Scouts
    Sublett's participation while growing up in the 1930s in Illinois, 77-79

Camp Robert Smalls
    Site of training for black enlisted men at Great Lakes, Illinois, during World War II, 11-17, 106-110; site of training for the first black officer candidates in early 1944, 25, 27-44, 124-143

Citizens Military Training Camp
    Provided military training for civilian teenagers at Fort Riley, Kansas, during the 1930s, 12, 92-96

Cooper, George C.
    Golden Thirteen member who went through the officer training program in early 1944 and was a knowledgeable educator, 34-35; Navy recruiting in recent years, 64;

service during World War II at Naval Training School, Hampton, Virginia, 111, 149-150

Dille, Lieutenant (junior grade) John F., Jr., USNR
As battalion commander at the Naval Training Station, Great Lakes, Illinois, was involved with the training of black officer candidates in early 1944, 27, 42-43

Downes, Commander Edwin H., USNR (USNA, 1920)
As head of the Naval Training School at Hampton, Virginia, during World War II, he took a sincere interest in black enlisted men, 26-27, 47-48, 113-118

Education
Sublett was in grade school and high school in Illinois in the 1920s and 1930s, 5-7, 70-72, 79-80, 86-90; Sublett attended three different colleges--Wisconsin, Northwestern, and George Williams--in the late 1930s and early 1940s, 8-9, 90-91, 97-98, 102-103

Eniwetok, Marshall Islands
Served as a staging site for ships and war materials being gathered for the planned invasion of Japan in 1945, 52-55, 160-169

Federal Bureau of Investigation
Sublett had no qualms about having his background checked by the FBI when he was being considered as a potential officer candidate in 1943, 129-130

Football
Sublett played in high school in the mid-1930s, 71; Sublett played at the University of Wisconsin in the late 1930s, 2, 99-101; Graham Martin played semipro ball under an assumed name in San Francisco in 1944, 48-49

Fort Riley, Kansas
Site of Citizens Military Training Camp for civilian teenagers during the 1930s, 12, 92-96

George Williams College, Chicago, Illinois
School attended briefly by Sublett in the early 1940s, 8

Golden Thirteen
Black enlisted men who were trained to be naval officers at Great Lakes, Illinois, in early 1944, 25, 27-32, 41-44, 124-143; Sublett's evaluations of individual members of the group, 33-41; no graduation ceremony in connection with the commissioning in March 1944, 45-46, 143-146; recognition for the achievements of the Golden Thirteen has come relatively recently, 46-47, 68, 175; none of the group was in combat in World War II, 56, 146-147; involvement in navy recruiting in recent years, 62-66; reunions of the group in 1977 and subsequently, 63, 176-181; dedication in 1987 of a building at Great Lakes in honor of the group, 197-199

Goodwin, Reginald E.
　　Member of the Golden Thirteen who went through the officer training program in early 1944 and was an attorney, 35

Great Lakes Naval Training Station, Great Lakes, Illinois
　　See Naval Training Station, Great Lakes, Illinois

Hair, James E.
　　Member of the Golden Thirteen who went through the officer training program in early 1944, 35; reunited with the rest of the Golden Thirteen survivors on board the USS Kidd (DDG-993) in 1982, 180-181

Integration
　　See Racial Integration

Johnson, Warrant Officer Louis, USNR
　　Served with Sublett on board a yard oiler based at San Francisco in 1945, 159-160

Joseph Dickman, USS (APA-13)
　　Transported various personnel from San Francisco to Hawaii in mid-1945, 170-171

Kidd, USS (DDG-993)
　　Ship that served as the site of a Golden Thirteen reunion in April 1982, 63, 180-181

Lear, Charles B.
　　Member of the Golden Thirteen who went through the officer training program in early 1944, was a strong leader but later committed suicide, 35-36, 136

Marshall Islands
　　See Eniwetok, Marshall Islands

Martin, Graham E.
　　Golden Thirteen member who went through the officer training program in early 1944 and was an outstanding football player and teacher, 36-37; played football under an assumed name while serving in San Francisco in 1944, 48-50

Naval Training School, Hampton, Virginia
　　Site of rate training for black enlisted men during World War II, 17-20, 47-48, 110-119, 147-151; Commander Edwin H. Downes, head of the school, took a sincere interest in black enlisted men, 26-27, 113-118

Naval Training Station, Great Lakes, Illinois
　　Site of recruit training for black enlisted men during World War II, 11-17, 106-110; site of officer training for the Golden Thirteen in early 1944, 25, 27-44, 124-143; site of training in venereal disease prevention in

1945, 52, 161-162; dedication in 1987 of a building at Great Lakes in honor of the Golden Thirteen, 197-199

Nelson, Dennis Denmark II
Golden Thirteen member who liked to be the center of attention while going through officer training in early 1944, 38-40, 108; served in stevedore battalion on Eniwetok in the Marshall Islands in 1945, 162, 164, 166-169; brought the Golden Thirteen together for a reunion in 1977, 176-177, 181-184

Northwestern University, Evanston, Illinois
School attended briefly by Sublett around 1940, 8

Officer Candidate School
Members of the Golden Thirteen received officer training in segregated Camp Robert Smalls at Great Lakes, Illinois, in early 1944, 25, 27-44, 124-143

Queen of Peace (A-45)
Converted fishing boat in which Sublett served in the Boston area in 1943, 21-22, 119-120

Racial Integration
Sublett was one of very few blacks in his high school class in Illinois in the late 1930s, 6-7, 70, 83-84; integrated crew of converted fishing boat and machine shop in the Boston area in 1943, 20-24, 119-123

Racial Prejudice
Some enlisted men did not salute the first black naval officers in 1944-45, but it was partly a matter of ignorance, not realizing they were officers, 44, 51, 150-151

Racial Segregation
Black enlisted men underwent recruit training at Camp Robert Smalls, Great Lakes, Illinois, during World War II, 11-17, 106-110; all-black rate training at the Naval Training School, Hampton, Virginia, during World War II, 17-20, 26-27, 47-48, 110-119, 147-151; training of the first black naval officers at Great Lakes, Illinois, in early 1944, 25, 27-41, 124-143; all-black stevedore battalion on Eniwetok in the Marshall Islands in 1945, 52-55, 160-169; races lived separately in Tennessee when Sublett was growing up, 72-73; Sublett lived in a private home when he was stationed in San Francisco in 1944-45 because the navy quarters were off limits, 153-155

Reagan, John W.
Golden Thirteen member who underwent officer training in early 1944 and was the best man at Sublett's wedding, 40

Recruiting, Navy
   Involvement on the part of the Golden Thirteen in recent years to attract minority personnel to the Navy, 62-66, 177-181

Reed, Lieutenant (junior grade) George W., USNR
   Served as officer in charge of a stevedore battalion on Eniwetok, Marshall Islands, in 1945, 39-40, 162-163, 168

Segregation
   See Racial Segregation

Smith, Warrant Officer Sidney M., USNR
   Served as a warrant machinist on Eniwetok, Marshall Islands, in 1945, then traveled to the United States with Sublett, 57-58, 163

Sublett, Eugenia Beck
   Married Frank Sublett, Jr., in 1944 and was later divorced from him in 1959, 56-57, 103-104, 140-141, 173

Sublett, Frank E., Sr.
   Worked in a variety of jobs prior to his death in 1956, 3-4, 90; was a capable football player as a young man, 73-74

Sublett, Frank E., Jr.
   Boyhood in Tennessee and Illinois in the 1920s and 1930s, 1, 4-6, 69, 73, 75-82; played football at the University of Wisconsin in the late 1930s, 2; attempted to join the Army Air Forces early in World War II, 3, 10, 96; parents, 3-6, 73-74, 80-81; church participation, 5; education in Illinois in the 1920s and 1930s, 5-7, 70-72, 79-80, 86-90; college education at Wisconsin, Northwestern, and George Williams in the late 1930s and early 1940s, 8-9, 90-91, 97-98, 102-103; worked in a variety of jobs as a youth, 4, 9, 76, 90-91; enlisted in the Navy in 1942 and took recruit training at Great Lakes, Illinois, 10-17, 106-110; attended Army-sponsored Citizens Military Training Camp at Fort Riley, Kansas, as a teenager, 12, 92-96; training as a machinist's mate at Hampton, Virginia, 17-20, 26-27; served on board a patrol craft and in a machine shop in the Boston area in 1943, 20-24, 119-123, 136-137; underwent officer training at Great Lakes, Illinois, in early 1944, 25, 27-44, 124-143; commissioning of in March 1944, 45-46, 143-146; served again at Hampton, Virginia, following commissioning, 47-48, 147-151; served in a patrol craft based in San Francisco in 1944-45, 48-49, 153-158; served in a yard oiler based in San Francisco in 1945, 50-51, 158-160; served as executive officer of a stevedore battalion on Eniwetok in 1945, 52-55, 160-169; married first wife, Eugenia, in 1944 and was subsequently divorced from her in 1959, 56-57; transition to civilian life following release from

active duty in 1946, 56-59, 103-104, 170-171; work in automobile dealer service departments from 1946 to 1980, 59, 61-62, 171-172; work as a professional model since 1980, 59-60, 186-192; participation in Boy Scouts while growing up, 77-79; limited social life while growing up, 83-84; Sublett has a great fondness for the out-of-doors, 84-86, 105; children of, 174-176; retirement activities in recent years, 192-195

Sublett, Frank III
Son of Frank Sublett, Jr., has worked in laboratories, 174-175

Sublett, Michael
Son of Frank Sublett, Jr., is a musician, 174-175

Sublett, Nicole
Daughter of Frank Sublett, Jr., is a house mother, 174

Taylor, Rosa S.
Frank Sublett's mother worked as a cook and companion, divorced from Sublett's father in 1931, 3-6, 73-74, 80-81

Sublett, Rosanne
Daughter of Frank Sublett, Jr., is a law school student, 174

Training
Black enlisted men went through boot camp at segregated Camp Robert Smalls, Great Lakes, Illinois, during World War II, 11-17, 106-110; rate training at Naval Training School, Hampton, Virginia, during World War II, 17-20, 26-27, 47-48, 110-119, 147-151; the Golden Thirteen were trained as naval officers at Great Lakes, Illinois, in early 1944, 25, 27-44, 124-143; training in venereal disease prevention at Great Lakes in 1945, 52, 161-162

Venereal Disease
Training in VD prevention at Great Lakes, Illinois, in 1945, 52, 161-162

White, William Sylvester
Golden Thirteen member who practiced law before undergoing naval officer training in early 1944, 40-41; Navy recruiting work in recent years, 64

Williams, Lewis R.
Naval enlisted man who went through officer training with the Golden Thirteen in early 1944 but was not commissioned, 41-42, 108

Wisconsin, University of, Madison, Wisconsin
Sublett attended and played football in the late 1930s, 2, 8-9, 97-101

www.ingramcontent.com/pod-product-compliance
Lightning Source LLC
Chambersburg PA
CBHW080613170426
43209CB00007B/1419